The Agile Project Manager 2020

How to blend traditional Project Management with an Agile methodology

DAVID B. TWILLEY, PMP, CSM

THE AGILE PROJECT MANAGER 2020
© **Month 2016**
By **David B. Twilley, PMP, CSM**

All rights reserved. No part of this book may be reproduced, stored in a retrieval system, or transmitted in any form or by any means, electronic, mechanical, photocopying, recording, scanning, or otherwise, without the prior written permission of the publisher except for the use of brief quotations in a book review.

ISBN-13: 978-1530433360
ISBN-10: 1530433363

Printed in the United States of America
First Printing, 2016

Free Download -- BOOK REVIEW REQUEST:

For those of you who downloaded this book either for free or at a reduced price, please help get the word out about our book.

If you enjoyed this book and found it useful, which hopefully you did, please spread the word and let everyone know how much you enjoyed it.

If you post a (mostly) positive review on Amazon, Goodreads, or other reputable location, please email us the following information and we will provide you a set of **100 PMP Exam sample questions** for free, plus our sincere appreciation.

Thank you all in advance.

Email the following details to

BookReviews@True-SpiritConsulting.com

Review Location:

Review Text:

Name:

E-Mail Address:

Thanks yet again and I hope you enjoy the book and learned something useful.

David B. Twilley

True Spirit Consulting

Contents

Prologue: What Is The Agile Project Manager 2020?	1
Chapter 1: Changing Perceptions of Project Management	7
Chapter 2: What Makes a Great Project Manager?	17
Chapter 3: Traditional Projects: The Waterfall Model	29
The Waterfall Five Project Phases:	37
Chapter 4: Agile Software Development	65
Chapter 5: Which Project Management Methodology	91
Evaluating The Project Pipeline:	98
Chapter 6: Outsourcing 2020	101
Chapter 7: Communication Plan 2020	117
Chapter 8: Building The Perfect Team	131
Chapter 9: Agile Project Management 2020	149
Chapter 10: Getting Your Company To Evolve Slowly	159
Chapter 11: Putting It All Together	169
Chapter 12: Conclusion	193
Appendix 1: "Running The Perfect Meeting"	197
Appendix 2: Project Methodology Answers	209
Appendix 3: Specific Project Types	213
Appendix 4: Professional Certifications	221
Appendix 5: How Not To Run A Meeting	227
Appendix 6: Sample Documents	229
Glossary Of Terms	233
Index	263
Book Review Request:	265
About The Author:	266

Prologue: What Is The Agile Project Manager 2020?

This will be that introductory chapter for those who like to skim books to see if there is anything in there worth reading. Well, in this one there absolutely is and we will tell you some of those features here.

In this book, we simplify some of the concepts around Agile, Scrum, Waterfall and all of the conversation in regards to which methodology is best and which should be used and which should not be. In our opinion, the answer to which methodology to use is simple: *use whichever methodology is most appropriate for your projects.*

We strongly recommend the adoption of Agile methodologies for the majority of all software development projects. We also feel the need to have a strong PMO Manager and Project Manager engaged, even for strictly Agile projects. This idea is contrary that of a strict interpretation of Scrum.

Also, we have some differences in how we view the role of the Scrum Master. In Agile Project Management 2020, we envision the Scrum Master as a combination of traditional Scrum Master role and that of a Technical Lead.

In our experience, there is just too much down time otherwise and not really enough for the Scrum Master to do. Sure, they could serve as Scrum Master on multiple projects, like a Project Manager does, but we see better results having them work as part of a dedicated team.

Another difference in Agile Project Management 2020 is our view that Agile Project Management should include four key individuals all involved in the project management process all working together.

The four roles in Agile Project Management 2020 are:

- PMO Manager
- Project Manager
- Scrum Master
- Product Owner

This again differs with a standard Agile methodology, in which the Scrum Master and Product Owner are responsible for everything. In our experience, this does not work and we cite several reasons that this is the case.

Our view is designed to incorporate Agile and Scrum as a part of an enterprise project management strategy.

Our primary aim is to prepare a corporate project team to be able to handle multiple types of projects equally adeptly, and to be pragmatic enough to be able to apply the appropriate methodology to the appropriate project

To summarize our views fairly quickly, and to differentiate us from other methodologies and strategies out there, here are three differentiators for our project management approach.

"Elevator Summary" Of Agile Project Management 2020:

With Agile Project Management 2020, we want to take the best of both project management methodologies and incorporate them into our process while also making some improvements in the process based on real-world limitations:

So, at a high-level for Agile Project Management 2020, we recommend the following:

Slow and Constant Change – the move towards a new project management methodology should be phased, consistent and well-communicated. There should not be a shock to the business, nor should it be done without the approval and political buy-in of the business.

The goal should be for lasting change, and lasting change has to be incorporated slowly, otherwise the normal human nature resistance and pushback will follow against a change that is perceived as too swift and/or radical.

Combination Waterfall/Agile PMO – It is time to stop the knee-jerk reactions that companies have when they feel the need to do the next "cool" thing. Many companies hear how Agile works and assume that it can be incorporated quickly with no adverse impacts.

This is obviously not the case, and also it is very important to note that Agile is not appropriate for all projects.

It just isn't.

Our vision is that of a combined Waterfall and Agile PMO, with talented Project Managers that are adept at using both methodologies equally and a strong PMO manager or PMO who can identify the proper PM methodology for each project based upon its own requirements and needs.

Collaboration between Project Manager, Scrum Master, and Product Owner – In traditional Scrum, there is not a specific role for Project Managers. Instead, the Scrum Master functions in this role and works with the Product Owner to get the project done. In Agile Project Management 2020, we see a collaboration between three roles in which the Project Manager continues to do the Initiation and Planning phases of the project but then turns the Execution and Monitoring phases over to the Scrum Master and Product Owners.

Increased Technical Role for Scrum Master –Following traditional Scrum methodologies, a Scrum Master's time is very open except for the various meetings that they must attend. So the logical question follows: "what should they do with the rest of their time?"

In some shops, the expectation is for a Scrum Master to run multiple Scrums, but then that takes them away from one of their specified responsibilities which is to "protect the Scrum process"

We view it differently. We feel that the Scrum Master should function on one or maximum two projects and be a technical contributor as well as managing the Scrum process. The expectation should be that of say 40-50% of a normal team member, but there is no reason that a technical Scrum Master should not be able to contribute more to the team than running some meetings, talking to the Product Owner and protecting the Scrum process.

We see the Scrum Master as a role for strong technical people to aspire to, one which provides them additional responsibility while also utilizing their developed technical skills and enable them to continue to contribute technically.

Features Of This Book:

Some features of this book that are unique to others on the market today are the following:

Does not preach Agile as the universal answer to all projects

Puts examples in context of most companies

Provides case study to help illustrate the challenges and issues that companies face when adopting agile or making any other change.

Chapter 11 provides a full project lifecycle for an agile project and waterfall showing how and when the paths diverge and illustrating the first few sprints in the project

CASE STUDY:

True Spirit Software and Energy Corporation

In this book, we will conclude each chapter with the application of the lessons learned to our company, True Spirit Software and Energy Corporation.

True Spirit Software and Energy Corporation is an Energy Trading and Oil and Gas company that has diversified their business to produce and market energy trading software as well.

As such there I.T requirements include both internal and external users, and have varying demands as far as timing and require a diverse set of both business and technical expertise.

The idea for this case study is to give some real-world examples of the realistic issues that most, if not all, companies will face.

Some of it is intended to be a little out of the ordinary just for dramatic impact, but the great majority of the issues portrayed will be based partly on real experiences.

The idea for this is to attempt to put the rather dry material presented here in a more applicable and relatable context, such that it can be better envisioned how the Agile Project Management 2020 philosophy can be used in almost any company with a multitude of different personalities.

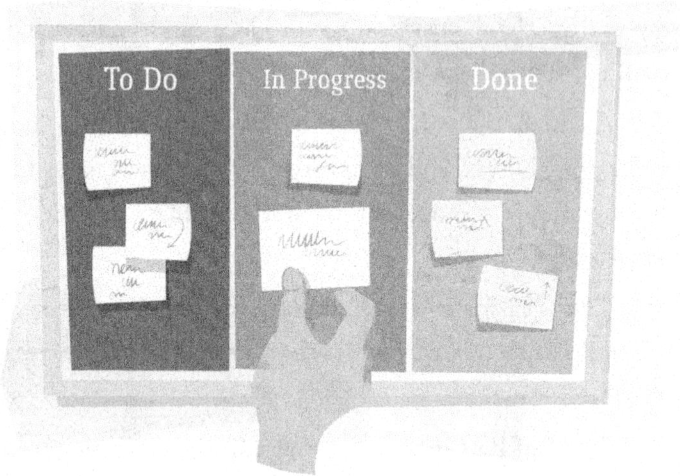
To Do
In Progress
Done

CHAPTER 1: Changing Perceptions of Project Management

"Project Management is only a necessary evil, and besides that it's boring."
--Former Client

I hear this all the time, and as both a Project Manager and a baseball coach I make the frequent comparison of project management to baseball, bear with me as I make the simple analogy.

Both baseball and project management can be *very* boring if you do not **understand** them. Once someone understands all of the details, everything that goes into being successful at it, the more interesting they become.

We strongly believe that Project Management should not be limited to creating Microsoft Project files and running status meetings. Project Managers should be engaging communicators involved in most if not all facets of the project.

David B. Twilley, PMP, CSM

"But, Project Managers don't serve any purpose, they only slow us down!"

I hear this frequently too, and that can be true in some circumstances. Some environments foster situations in which the Project Manager is nothing more than someone who builds a project plan and schedule and then walks around checking up on people every day to see how the project is progressing. These types of Project Managers create resentment within their teams, who then tend to cringe when the Project Managers approach.

A former colleague of mine once said: "if the project team is happy to see you when you come over, then you aren't doing your job as Project Manager".

Man, I could not **disagree** more.

I have worked in shops such as this, in which the Project Manager is a pariah, unwelcome in all circles and just generally not appreciated.

We envision a landscape, a culture in which the Project Manager is a contributing and welcomed member of a team, not a task master.

We believe that Project Management need not be boring, nor should the role of Project Manager be diminished to that of a paper shuffling, Gantt-chart loving, meeting-minute writing autocrat.

Maybe, just maybe, the role of Project Manager can be much more than that.

We envision an environment in which the Project Team is used more in a partner role rather than subjects over whom the Project Manager rules supreme.

In Agile Project Management 2020, we envision a new form of Project Management in which the Project Manager has a role, but also knows when to step out. We see a situation in which multiple project methodologies can be implemented under an overarching project strategy to optimize the entire team.

In our plan and vision, teams are developed for the long term, with opportunity for individual development and opportunities for growth.

We envision a combination of outsourcing and offshore with newer trends such as near shoring and using and developing junior resources.

We envision providing new roles for technical staff, and insisting that our Project Managers learn and understand the technology, at least at the most basic level.

And finally, for Agile projects we see roles for the Project Manager, Scrum Master, and Product Owner to work together. We don't feel that a traditional Project Manager should be converted to be either a Scrum Master or Product Owner. More on that in Chapter 3

So, please join us on our Project Management discussion. Hopefully, you will learn something along the way, and we hope to stimulate some discussions at your offices.

What is Agile Project Management 2020?

Agile PM 2020 is not a new beginning, but rather an **evolution** of the current Scrum/Agile model. At its core, it applies basic common sense to determine how to vary project management methodologies to better serve the project and also the project sponsor and users.

One key difference in AgilePM2020 is that we don't propose Agile as being appropriate for all projects. It depends on the project, the team, the due date, etc. Several factors might make a project unsuitable for an Agile strategy.

We clarify the role of the Project Manager, which in true Scrum models has been diminished. We reason that this is done only because the roles of the Scrum Master and Product Owner have been misunderstood.

In AgilePM2020, the Project Manager, Product Owner and Scrum Master all work together to initiate and plan the project, and then the Project Manager takes a "hands off" approach during the sprints to enable the Scrum Master and the team.

This way the Project Manager can focus on their strengths: planning, documentation and communication to the business and the Scrum Master and team can function without the need to provide daily or weekly updates to a Project Manager.

What is Project Management 2020?

Project Management 2020 is a discussion and analysis of the current project management methodologies and also our best guess as to which of these methodologies and approaches will be used in the future. We examine current PM methodologies such as Waterfall, Agile, and Scrum.

We also discuss the outsourcing trend and how this might change with the move to more on-site project development. Along the way, several Case studies will be provided to indicate what has and what has not worked for certain projects in the past. Our objective is to learn from those mistakes and move forward and improve.

What This Book is not:

This book is not an extensive primer or reference book intended to cover every facet of Project Management and every methodology ever used. Instead, we aim to focus on what has and has not worked from our experience and thus provide our wisdom to you the reader.

We will provide information for those seeking to pursue credentials and certifications such as the PMP, PMI-ACP or the Certified Scrum Master (CSM). We even touch briefly on other areas such as Six Sigma.

Who This Book is for and How to Use This Book:

If you are a beginning project manager, we feel that this book will be very beneficial to you as you begin your career in Project Management. We can help you focus on how to build your career and avoid some of the pitfalls of Project Management.

For more experienced project managers, we feel that this book will help you gain perspective and be forward-looking in your planning, and maybe help develop your career a little bit better. PMO Managers might especially find this book useful because of the ideas for managing a large program of Projects.

One of the key points that we will make is that not all projects should be managed the same way. For Managers and Stakeholders, this book can help you identify those techniques that are being used and also identify where you might be able to contribute more and be involved in the process earlier. As we will stress quite often in this book, Stakeholder involvement is critical in every phase of the project, not just the beginning and the end.

For Project Managers:

This discussion will be useful for Project Managers to see how things are done at different companies and consider different methodologies. A strict Agile or Scrum methodology devalues the role of the Project Manager, but for us, it is still a viable role, albeit different from a Waterfall role.

For PMO Managers:

This book will be useful for those looking to evaluate and consider Agile, but fear that it may be too drastic of a change for your enterprise. One of our key themes in this book is the fact that there is no one size fits all for every project. One of the most important things that a PMO Manager and Project Manager can do is to evaluate each specific project for its own needs and not become overly committed to any one project management methodology.

For Managers:

For managers, and specifically those on the business side, this book will help you to understand the overall concepts of Agile and see how they could benefit your organization. Benefits such as increased speed, better visibility, and more user involvement are key features of Agile and are strong selling points to many managers.

The general idea that development is done at an iterative level rather than planning every single step ahead of time, making changing it later very difficult.

Agile provides a quicker start and a more adaptable development environment, making it very easy to change priorities, and shift gears very quickly.

For Developers and Technical People:

Developers, Business Analysts and other technical team members should really like Agile. Agile provides the opportunity for the technical team to get out of the shadow of the Project Manager and lead the day-to-day operations.

They become valued partners in the process instead of simply resource cogs to be entered on a Gantt chart and managed like just any other type of commodity.

For others wanting to learn Project Management:

This book provides an excellent overview of the IT project Management process and discusses several current trends. For those of you who wish to get into Project Management, we feel that this is an excellent place to start.

So, that is our story, now to begin to discuss the basics of our ideas, let's talk about Agile Project Management 2020:

CASE STUDY:

True Spirit Software and Energy Corporation

True Spirit Software and Energy Corporation had the same Chief Information Officer for the last twenty years. The man known affectionately as "Bubba" was intelligent, outgoing, and almost universally loved by the IT department and business as well.

After his retirement, the company looked outside to hire a fresh face.

The company hired Patty Smith, a very ambitious, assertive executive recently having departed one of the major technology firms in Silicon Valley.

With all of her software and technology background, Ms. Smith is under the impression that Agile is the only way to go in regards to project management and has brought those values with her.

True Spirit is a completely Waterfall-Traditional project management shop, but Patty has vowed to change all of that, whether the existing teams like it or not.

The first order given upon assuming her new position as CIO, is to start to manage all applications using an Agile methodology starting immediately.

The task for the PMO manager is to determine the most appropriate projects to start on for the current year, build an ideal Agile team and also get buy-in by the business for the new process change.

Patty Smith calls the PMO Manager, Richard Thompson, into her office and explains the situation

"We need to have all of our projects managed with an agile methodology for the coming year," Patty says.

"I understand." Richard replies, "But can I ask exactly what you're thinking is behind this change."

"Well," Patty replies, "I was speaking with several colleagues of mine who work with software companies and software development and they almost universally praised agile as the way to go."

Richard hears this and in that single statement, he realizes his issue. In the mind of the new CIO agile is perfect and the unquestioned answer for software development.

But, as Richard thinks to himself, "We are not only a software company."

Thus begins Richard's challenge to determine the best course of action for all projects, and maintain political obedience such that he does not offend the new CIO.

Sounds like fun, right?

So, for the next few chapters join us as we look in on the special circumstances of True Spirit Software and Energy and see if we can learn from some of their mistakes and maybe also what they do well.

Before we get too much further, let us introduce the "cast members" if you will, of our little case study:
Refer to this for the remainder of our case study sections as it can get quite confusing.

NAME	ROLE
Patty Smith	Chief Information Officer (CIO)
Rob Johnson	Director
Rick Wilson	Director
Monique Richards	Director
Richard	PMO Manager
Bill	Project Manager
Craig	Project Manager
Steve	Project Manager
Mark	Project Manager
Minh	Project Manager
Bhaskal	Technical Lead – Scrum Master
Shawn	Technical Lead – Scrum Master
Linda	Technical Lead
Andrew	Architect
Donna	Developer
Dan	Developer
Juanita	Developer
Gustavo	Chile Team
Korina	Chile Team
Almendra	Chile Team

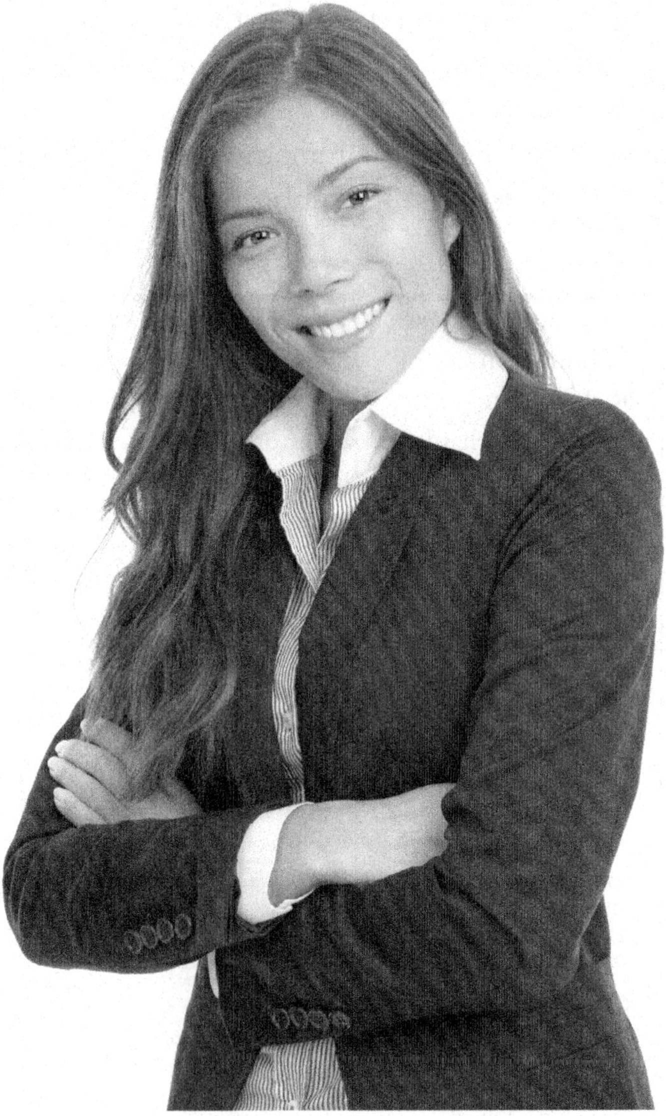

CHAPTER 2: What Makes A Great Project Manager?

"The only way to do great work is to love what you do."
--Steve Jobs

Project Management is an underappreciated skill. That might seem like an overstatement, but in many organizations, the understanding of what a Project Manager does, and what their responsibilities are differs greatly across the board.

Back to the earlier discussion in the introduction, in many ways project management is underappreciated because it is not fully understood. Too often individuals end up in project management that simply do not suit that job.

Just as a star technical performer might not be suitable for a management role, in the same way, not all people are ideal for a project management role, and this is something that is starting to be realized more and more.

What are the key components or attributes of a successful Project Manager?

A project manager must wear many hats and many times is simply the middleman between two parts of the company, and has to be the bearer of bad news, subject to "kill the messenger syndrome".

At various times, a Project Manager must be:

- Coach
- Administrative Assistant
- Planner
- Accountant
- Psychologist
- Public Speaker

So how does each specific roles/skills apply to the job of Project Manager? Well, let's discuss.

Coach

A good Project Manager needs to manage and motivate a team and apply strategy how to succeed with the resources that he has.

For those of you non-sports types this might not seem relevant, but having served as a baseball and soccer coach I can tell you the comparisons are apt. In both situations, groups must work together towards a single goal.

In both situations, there are star performers, average performers, and poor performers. And finally, in both situations, some of the average and poor performers can typically improve with more coaching and peer support.

Unfortunately, a few team members will never become good contributors and should be cut from the team.

There are also the normal human issues that make us all so very different. A good Project Manager must be able to understand these differences and realize the need to change their tactics to suit the individuals they are working with, whether this is the project team, customer or other stakeholders.

Administrator:

This point could be debated, but many times a Project Manager's job is like that of an Administrative assistant. An undeniable part of a Project

Manager's job is maintaining documentation, and acting in a deferential role to management, coordinating and planning meetings, working around other people's schedules.

Clearly, organizational skills are of paramount importance. If a Project Manager is not organized and does not stay one step ahead of the project team then a bad impression could be created.

Planner:

Another undeniable part of a Project Manager's life is the need to be a forward-looking planner. A good Project Manager is proactive, rather than reactive, but also has that innate ability to see into the future with some accuracy.

This means planning for contingencies, anticipating risks, and coordinating competing priorities and managing personal schedule conflicts.

Accountant:

Managing a budget can be a significant portion of a Project Manager's time. At my busiest point, I was managing budgets easily in the combined total of over 5 million.

Determining which costs are considered to be capital and which are expense, which period it should be charged in, etc are not typical skills held by most IT people. This accounting element is another challenge that Project Managers must deal with.

Psychologist:

Somewhat similar to being a coach, but part of a Project Manager's job is managing the individual personalities on their teams. This includes maintaining an individual relationship as well as managing interpersonal conflicts that may arise between various team members.

We will stress many times in the book about the importance of team, but it is also important that a Project Manager understand each individual on the team and understand that each person will respond differently and thus should be treated for their specific needs and valued for their specific skills.

Public Speaker:

And finally, the role that makes many of us uncomfortable.

Project Managers must be able to lead a room, whether in person or via telephone and command and lead the agenda.

For those with more passive, timid personalities this can be a difficult challenge.

Project Managers must be able to present ideas clearly in a multitude of situations such as Project Status Meetings, Project Kick-Off Meetings etc.

The ability to clearly and persuasively communicate to various types of audiences is a crucial Project Management skill.

Skills and Traits of a Successful Project Manager:

Project Managers need to have a combination of skills that enable them to take care of all steps required to get the job done.

Technical Skills

We touched upon this earlier but it is paramount that a project manager has the ability to understand what is being completed at a technical level.

For this reason, we believe that former developers and business analysts make good Project Managers because they come into the job with those technical skills already in place.

Business Knowledge

This is similar to technical skills, but even more important when discussing the project with the stakeholders. There is no realistic way that a Project

Manager can discuss the projects and truly understand the business impact and needs without comprehending the business.

A project manager that I worked with had taken a job with an Energy company with no real knowledge of the underlying industry.

For the first six months of the project, it was a complete struggle because he did not understand the needs of the refineries, nor did he grasp the needs of the traders which he supported.

Sure, he was able to manage schedules, communication and all of the other generic project management skills, but without this basic knowledge of the business, he was out of his element

The Four Key Abilities:

From our experience the successful Project Managers all have similar traits. Not in their personality, not in their looks, no they share the ability to do four things well.

A project manager should have the ability to do the following, and do the following WELL:

- Communicate
- Delegate
- Motivate
- Appreciate

Communicate:

We will stress this so much that our readers will get frustrated, but communication is the number one project management skill.

Communication is everywhere in the Project Manager's world. Whether it is communication with the team, communication with IT management, or communication with the stakeholders.

Communication, or the lack thereof, will make or break a project.

This is so important that we dedicate an entire chapter to this key point later in the book, our chapter Communication Management 2020.

One of the issues that I have seen over and over again are otherwise talented people who are in the role of Project Manager who are poor communicators.

Read it here first: this simply does not work.

I believe people can improve their communication. I am not suggesting that one must be as persuasive as a salesperson or as an attorney, but it is paramount that as a Project Manager, that you are heard, understood and "hopefully", respected as well.

Delegate:

Project Managers must have the ability to delegate tasks and communicate these responsibilities clearly to their team. A project manager needs to be careful not to over delegate and take care of a certain amount of tasks on their own.

When a task is delegated or assigned, the expectations must be clearly stated, ideally both verbally and also in some tangible method such as an email or another item that provides a paper trail.

Motivate:

At a certain point, a Project Manager needs to be able to take charge and not be a "nice guy". It is your responsibility to motivate the individuals on your team, even if you are in a matrix environment in which these people do not report to you.

A project manager needs to be able to command respect and get the team to work for them. Try to lead by example, show a real interest in what these people do, and try to be someone that people want to do well for.

One of the most delicate balancing acts that a Project Manager must face is the balance of earning the respect of the team while also being liked by them. In this case, it is FAR more important to be respected than be liked.

Sometimes the well-liked nice guys are the ones team members feel they can take advantage of.

Appreciate:

If the team performs above and beyond expectations be sure to recognize their efforts.

This is when the coaching facet is involved, we need to be sure to be just as supportive and appreciative as we are demanding and professional.

People want to work hard for people they like and respect, there is no need to be an autocratic jerk. Strive to be the person that you would want to work for yourself.

In my experience, the most successful managers and project managers are those you respect first and like second.

Don't think for a minute that a team will work hard for you if they hate you, sure they may work for you, but they will hold something back.

Be the "Bad Guy":

Another way that we as Project Managers can show appreciation is by demonstrating that we have the backs of our team members.

One of the most difficult facets of Project Management is that many times you have to be the one delivering the bad news. A project manager should not point out an under-performing team member and site them as the reason that a date was missed.

This falls on the Project Manager, as unfair as it may be. Also, a Project Manager has the responsibility of resisting a user request if it falls outside of the project parameters.

We recommend having some built-in flexibility in the timeline just for such an occurrence. But, for example, if a key stakeholder requests a large new feature one week before the go-live date, it is the **Project Manager's job** to inform this stakeholder that it cannot be done in the time allotted.

Another example from a former client, I worked with a project manager who had a deadline less than two weeks away. A revised requirement came in and she did not want to approve it because it was so close to the deadline.

Unknown to her, her boss had already promised this feature to the client without her knowledge and had overruled her on pushing back to the client.

When the deadline was subsequently missed because there was not really adequate time to complete, it was the Project Manager and not the boss that approved the change that got in trouble.

Yeah, didn't really seem fair to me either.

In our vision of Project Management, a Project Manager is very important, but several people will need to change their view of what a Project Manager's responsibilities are.

We envision Project Managers who are technically savvy, adaptable, and willing to work as a partner with others on the team to make projects successful.

We see Project Managers who are equally comfortable with Waterfall as they are with Agile. The knowledge of both is very important to be adaptable enough to apply different methodologies to different projects.

And finally, we envision Project Managers who focus on their communication and will make this their number one priority. By combining different communication methods, the Project Manager should engage stakeholders early; apply their observations and analysis to determine the specific communication needs for each stakeholder.

In our vision, the Project Manager role is not going away, but it is evolving. Like anything else, for those individuals willing to adapt, they will likely be successful.

On the other hand, those unwilling to adapt might need to consider other career alternatives or take a different path.

We strongly feel that the Project Manager role needs to evolve, partly out of necessity. Several Agile and Scrum environments either remove or diminish the role of the Project Management role.

Next we will discuss the basics of the Waterfall and Agile methods, and then discuss the Agile Project Manager 2020 idea to incorporate all of this into one successful enterprise strategy.

David B. Twilley, PMP, CSM

CASE STUDY:

True Spirit Software and Energy Corporation

The new mandate has been provided and the PMO Manager must determine the best way to implement Agile into the organization.

To do this, first he must inform his team of Project Managers of this change, and hope that this idea goes over well with the team.

With his current team of four project managers, he realizes that he already has two that have been cross-trained with Agile, one has their Certified Scrum Master credential and one other has his PMI-ACP credential.

He doesn't expect to have any issues with them, but it's the other two Project Managers that concern him.

One of them, Steve, is a very non-technical, by the book Waterfall project manager who has been in Project Management for over twenty years.

Mark, the other, is a more dictatorial type Project Manager, one who feels that a Project Manager should not only lead but also sort of *rule* over a Project.

Richard, the PMO lead, is not so sure how well this will work.

To address these issues quickly, Richard calls a meeting with the four project managers: Bill, Craig, Steve and Mark.

After about thirty minutes discussing the new mandate, Richard opens up the floor for questions.

"How will this impact the existing Project Managers?" Steve asks as he is the one most reluctant to change.

"In the short term, there will be no change," Richard replies, "We will, however, want all of our Project Managers to get the proper training on Agile."

"This sounds like some bullshit to me," Steve says, in his normally charming manner, "I have heard that with Agile there **are** no project managers. They use these things called Scum Managers or something."

"That's Scrum *Master*, genius," Bill adds, countering Steve's lack of information.

"Hold on, both of you," Richard says, "to address your question, Steve, that is a good point. Actually, in traditional Agile, the role of Project Manager is either secondary or eliminated altogether."

"What the hell!?" Steve exclaims.

"Hold up, a minute." Richard says, "but we are not doing that here."

"For **now** maybe," Steve replies, sarcastically.

"No, smartass, forever," Richard replies, "This was part of the conditions discussed with Patty and me when I agreed to do this."

Steve doesn't respond, but his facial expression makes it obvious that he is not convinced.

"What about training opportunities?" Craig asks, "What specific opportunities are there?"

"Good question, Craig," Richard replies, "We are looking at a few options. The Certified Scrum Master course or the PMI-ACP course, depending on the role."

"Are we all going to be trained to be Scrum Masters?" Bill asks.

Richard hesitates and then responds, "I would prefer that we not be Scrum Masters, and maintain our role as PM. If some of you have an interest in this, I will support it. But my primary position is that there should be a PM working with a Scrum Master supporting each other."

"Mark, one thing you might not like," Richard says, "is that the PM now is not in charge of the day to day operations of the project."

"No," Mark says, "I cannot say that I like that at all."

CHAPTER 3: Traditional Projects: The Waterfall Model

"Of all the things I've done, the most vital is coordinating the talents of those who work for us and pointing them towards a certain goal"
-Walt Disney

The Current Project Management Landscape:

What does a current project look like? Well if you are like me, you have seen a lot of successful projects as well as some that completely collapsed.

Typically we see projects that are poorly planned and rushed into production, or the opposite of this where projects are over planned and stakeholders get frustrated and give up.

Software Development is expected to grow by 40% in the next five years. The question is how exactly will projects be led, managed and coordinated.

This is our objective here to determine exactly what the best plan should be moving forward into the next decade.

Before we discuss Agile in greater detail, let's discuss the "Traditional" methodology for managing the majority of projects which is known as the "Waterfall" methodology.

Waterfall is so named because it follows a structured, linear process that involves a great deal of planning up front and a slow start. One of its primary objectives is to cover and identify as many possible issues in the Initiating and Planning phases, such that the Execution becomes fairly straightforward.

Agile differs with that in that it allows for more changes, whereas Waterfall is mostly locked in once the Planning phase is completed. This makes incorporating changes less dynamic.

If, as a reader, you are not interested in the basics of the Waterfall methodology, feel free to skip over this chapter and proceed to the other more interesting chapters.

It pains me to admit it, but this one is rather dull. Not the writing, that is of course riveting, but the subject matter itself.

The Waterfall Methodology: Project Management Process Groups:

An overview of the basic project management process groups

- Initiating
- Planning
- Executing
- Controlling/Monitoring
- Closing

Let's first discuss the Project Management knowledge areas, and then we will move in to discuss the specifics of each of the Project Management Processes in the Waterfall model

Project Management Knowledge Areas:

Within the process groups, many management types comprise the full management of a project. PMBOK defines these specialized management skills as *knowledge areas*. Each knowledge area is present in at least two of each of the process groups.

Knowledge Areas:
Scope Management

Scope management revolves around defining the work that will and will not be included as part of the project. Managing scope requires that you identify and document the requirements necessary to make the project a success.

We will discuss the multiple approaches to defining scope that can be taken when planning a project. One of the key points of the book (which we intend to make anyway) is that scope should be the most flexible area of any project. When projects start, there are many situations in which the scope simply cannot be all defined at once. Not because the Project Manager does not have the ability, but rather the stakeholders don't yet know exactly what they want.

For this reason, we feel that scope management is one of the most important facets of any project and the one that should have the most latitude and flexibility during the project.

Cost Management:

During planning, the cost of project work is estimated. These costs include materials, other resources and labor costs. From these costs, a budget can be constructed and defined.

From here, as the work progresses, the status of the project is monitored and we compare the budget to the amount spent.

Time Management:

Typically when a project starts, the stakeholders provide a due date. This due date is not necessarily a so-called "drop dead date" but rather say a quarterly target or some other customer-dictated date.

Sometimes there are fixed dates that simply must be met, say for example for federal tax compliance, before the end of a quarter for reporting purposes etc. From this defined date, a project manager must put time management into practice. This is defined by generating the project schedule.

Tasks need to be defined and then must be estimated and scheduled. Here is where certain project methodologies differ with their planning methods. In traditional waterfall, these tasks are defined, estimated and scheduled in a linear, Gantt chart method and followed in a straightforward manner.

Agile project management involves different scheduling approaches, by which tasks are estimated by effort and then planned into two-week sprints as selected by the team. We will discuss this in greater detail later, but this is how we see Agile as being more advantageous, as it enables the team to participate in the estimating and planning progress.

By being more involved, typically estimates are a great deal more accurate and the team members also feel more engaged in the process.

Once the project is underway, the Project Manager must monitor progress and take steps necessary to control the schedule.

Human Resource Management:

As part of the planning process, once the tasks are estimated, the skills and roles are identified that will be required to complete said tasks. This staffing plan is developed and then added to the project.

In our opinion, the Project Manager should be very involved in the selection of the team members and understand the abilities and strengths/weaknesses of each potential team member.

The Importance of Team:

There is one key point to make here, which we will elaborate on later in the book. Next to stakeholder communication, we feel that engaging the team and creating a feeling of team unity is the most important responsibility of the Project Manager.

Few things are more motivating that belonging to a group that works together seamlessly towards the same goal. This can be very difficult to do, but should be one of the areas in which Project Managers focus their time.

Be Part of the Team:

Now the balancing act that all Project Managers must face: how can we lead the team while being a contributing part of it at the same time? This is for those of you Project Managers who are not that technical, but may be managing a technical project.

One key piece of advice is to, at least, **understand** the technology enough to both speak to it and to understand what is being discussed.

I have worked with several Project Managers who were assigned very, very technical projects to manage. One of my former colleagues, Mark, was so non-technical that he had difficulty simply accessing tools on which to record status reports. This was ok for a while until he started managing complex software development projects for a key company initiative.

On this project, some of the developers on his team would snicker behind his back because they felt that they could tell him any type of technical B.S and he would not have a single clue that they were lying to him. This lack of respect plagued the project and ultimately it was unsuccessful.

Project Managers need to become technically proficient at least enough to understand what is being said. I remember my first infrastructure project when the architects were discussing the difference between Virtual Machines and physical servers and details such as this.

I felt completely uncomfortable, but performed my due diligence, did some research and then for the next meeting I was able to add some valuable comments or ,at least, comment on something without completely sounding stupid while doing it.

The key point here is that by not understanding the technology involved in the project it sends an unintentional message to the team either that the PM is too good to need to understand the technology or that he or she doesn't care enough about it to learn to speak about it. Obviously, either of these two perceptions is not positive.

Procurement Management/Sourcing:

This most often refers to a situation in which a purchase is needed such as a software system. This can also refer to the process of obtaining outsourced or contract workers for the project if the in-house resources are deemed either unavailable or insufficient for the project at hand.

More often than not, this process will involve a separate department that helps to work with the vendors and take care of details such as the request for quotations, request for proposals and then the vendor evaluation process.

I have had several projects, however, where the Project Manager and the Stakeholders had the discretion and liberty to manage all of this themselves, and then would simply bring in the Sourcing department at the end to manage the paperwork and then legal to do the contract negotiations.

Communication Management:

As we will continue to stress in this book, we feel that Communication is the key responsibility of a project manager. This includes the communication with the project team, and equally important is the communication with the stakeholders and the project sponsor(s).

The Communication Plan is one key component of project communication, but we recommend that Project Managers develop a skill to have the flexibility to deviate from this plan based upon the personality types of the stakeholders on the specific project.

Once a communication plan is finalized, you may see that for some projects everyone is quite comfortable with the plan and that no issues arise. Other projects seem to have that one stakeholder who needs more assurance, more frequent updates and that warm and fuzzy feeling that the project is proceeding as planned.

One of my key lessons learned in project management is that not everyone is an optimist. I always firmly believed that unless I said anything to the contrary, people would know that the project was on schedule, everything was fine and there were no issues.

Well, quite the opposite is true. Without constant reassurances and reminders, people start to get nervous, and unfortunately, tend to assume the worst unless they are constantly reassured and comforted.

You should always over-communicate as opposed to under communicate. I am not sure why, but nothing creates more resentment and misunderstandings than failing to clearly communicate project status consistently and almost on a daily basis.

Quality Management:

Quality control represents measuring and recording the results of quality activities you can use to test your deliverables. An aspect of quality assurance is ensuring that the quality of your project complies with the standards defined by your organization.

Here is where some quality control mechanism could be applied to help eliminate consistent errors that are occurring across the enterprise. We advise Six Sigma, details of which will be discussed later in this book

Risk Management:

What is a Risk? A risk is defined as an event that has some probability of occurring in the future. A risk need not be negative, but we typically don't have to worry too much about positive risks, since a change to the positive won't typically create problems.

We identify risk management with three processes although many claim it to be four. These processes are identified as follows:

- Recognize risks and assess the probability of occurrence
- Differentiate between risks and issues. Remember a Risk is defined as something that **may** occur, whereas an Issue is something that **has** happened.
- Develop Risk Responses
- Monitor and respond to Risks

THE WATERFALL FIVE PROJECT PHASES:

The Initiation Phase:

The Initiation process group is the first of five PMBOK defined project process groups. The initiation processes formalize the authorization to start a project. Remember also that process groups can apply to both a new project and a new phase of an existing project.

Most projects I have worked on have not required this, but it can happen.

At the beginning of a project, the Initiation processes link the project's business needs to the project. Clear business goals and objectives are developed and tied to the rationale for the projects need. Basic budget estimates are defined and the project team is identified.

The project scope is examined first in the initiation phase and key structural decisions are made about how the project will be planned and executed.

Project Initiation Stage Major Outputs

Project Initiation will be consistent regardless of which Project Management methodology is chosen. The execution might be different, but the steps leading up to this are all fairly consistent.

Initiation phases should involve asking the questions to determine what is being addressed by this project.

There exist two major outputs from the Project Initiation Phase:

- Project Charter
- Preliminary Project Scope Statement

This analysis should be done even prior to the completion of the project charter.

Key Points in the Initiation Phase:

Problem Statement – What is the problem?

Project Objective – What is the purpose/objective of the project?

Project Scope -- What will the project do and not do

Success Criteria – This is likely the most important factor. What makes the project successful? This criterion should be defined by the business stakeholders and internal customers if there are any. As we have learned from many past projects, what defines a successful project can vary from time to time.

Problem Statement – problem statement should not state a solution but rather simply note the situation that exists and the opportunity for improvement

Project Goal – The goal statement is the opposite of the problem statement. The Goal statement is the intended outcome of the project.

The goal statement should be phrased in a positive manner and describe the "To-Be" objectives of the project. One way to think of the difference between the problem statements as just that, the Problem statement is the "as is" description of the current existing problem.

The goal statement is the envisioned perfection of the "to be" future vision, and that which hopefully this project will resolve.

Example Problem Statement:

Problem Statement	**Goal Statement**
Website does not properly persist user login information across pages because log in information is stored client side	Login information should be available and visible on each page in which the user has logged in.

Project Objectives:

The project objectives are explicitly designed objectives that flesh out the vague goals defined in the goal statement.

When these objectives have been accomplished, the goal is considered to be completed.

Whereas a goal statement should be fairly vague and not prescribe a necessary solution, the project objectives should be far more specific.

I feel that this acronym is somewhat overused (as are many in our business) but at this point this acronym is particularly appropriate so we will continue to use it.

The acronym for the project objectives is SMART

(Specific, Measurable, Assignable, Realistic, and Time-Based)

Specific – define what is going to be done. Again, specific so a significant amount of detail should be visible here.

Measurable – some way to quantify progress and completion

Assignable – the objective needs to be something that can be assigned to either an individual or a team.

Realistic – a project objective needs to be something that realistically can be completed. No project objectives such as re-designing the 1980's SDI program and putting lasers back into space. Time Travel is also not allowable here.

Time-Based—objective must be something that can have a time deadline attached to it.

The following are key project documents that are likely required regardless of the methodology that is chosen:

Project Charter:

The Project Charter is the key project document for a project. It can be a two-page summary or it can be a fifty-page mini book. We recommend that the Project Charter be a document that is **static** once the project initiation phase is completed.

We have worked at other clients that continue to modify the project charter multiple times with detail after detail but we feel this is the role of the Project Plan.

Remember the charter should initiate the project, and the Project Plan should contain the information in the planning phase. The charter, if following guidelines strictly, should be completed and filed away at the end of the Initiation phase.

The subject areas that the project charter addresses include the following:

Business Issues – these include the risks, assumptions, costs and ROI for the project

Expected Results – Description of the product, feature, or service that the project is expected to deliver.

Scope – this should be a rough identification of the objectives. Details will not be at this point. There does need to be enough information that basic time and cost estimates can be provided

Key Requirements In The Project Charter Are:

- Business Case
- Project Description
- Project Manager and Key Team Members
- Constraints
- Assumptions
- Project Management Methodology (**AgilePM2020 Modification)

Note here that we have added the need to put PM Methodology in the Project Charter. In our ideal Project Management process, it is during this Initiation phase, the time in which the Project Charter is written that we identify the specific Project Management methodology for the project.

So, again with the project charter, during the Initiation phase, enough details need to be provided in order to begin the project. The Charter should have this initial amount of detail and then for the planning phase be extended accordingly.

During the planning phase, some clients continue to modify this document and create multiple versions of this. We actually have seen more success and especially audit compliance by making the charter static and finished at the end of the Initiation phase.

From the beginning of the Planning Phase, the Project Plan should be the focus instead of the Project Charter.

In our example on the next page, our project charter is envisioned as being a charter purely for the Initiation phase. Detailed project plans are more relevant for Waterfall projects, so will not be provided here even though this is a discussion of the Waterfall methodology.

See Appendix 7 In The Back For A Free Sample Project Charter

Preliminary Project Scope Statement

A Preliminary Project Scope Statement provides a high-level scope narrative. Usually, the requirements are only vaguely defined at this point. The scope should include items that are both in and OUT of scope to alleviate any potential future misunderstandings.

Key Components Of The Preliminary Project Scope Statement:

Project Description

Explain what the project is, and how it will be accomplished. Explain the ultimate intended outcome of the project. This should serve as a brief introduction. Provide some background about the history of how the project got to this point.

Project Purpose

State the purpose of the project. Tie the purpose to the organization's strategic goals and objectives if possible. Tell the reader why this project is being started and what need it is fulfilling. Identify if there are any specific mandates, policies or laws that are driving this change.

Project Objectives

Provide clear, actionable and measurable objectives of the project. The objectives should be clear enough so that the project can be measured against the objectives once completed. The ultimate success of a project is whether the project achieved its stated objectives. Take time to clearly document the objectives here.

An example of an objective is:

The system/product/service will cut response times in half, thus allowing the organization to process twice as many tickets.

Project Requirements

Identify the high-level, important requirements of the product or service that will be developed. Remember that this is not a detailed list of system requirements or specifications at this point. The requirements might be at a level that is sufficient for performing an alternatives analysis to identify vendors and service providers that can meet the requirements.

An example of a requirement is:

The system will provide users with the ability to create and maintain a login account and profile online.

If you have elicited enough requirements where it makes sense to group the requirements by category, then feel free to display the requirements by category. Generally, there are two types of requirements: functional and non-functional. Non-functional requirements are generally broken into groups like security, usability, quality, scalability, privacy, maintainability, etc.

Project Assumptions

Assumptions are conditions at the start of the project that must be considered. For example, when developing the new software system that is going to take 3 years to fully complete, an assumption could be that the project budget is approved each year for three years so that the project scope is not impacted.

Project Constraints

Constraints are situations or events on the ground that must be considered and accounted, for which the project has no control over. For example, a constraint can be a hard deadline or completion date. Other constraints could be resources, tools or hardware -- so that if the project has no budget for additional servers, then the project must find a way to develop the new system using the hardware already in place.

This could mean juggling servers to fit specific development environment needs while ensuring that the production environment stays up.

Project Boundaries

If the product or system boundary is known, describe it here. For example, if a system requires access to multiple external systems (e.g., a system of systems), then it might make sense to break the scope of work into multiple phases so that the scope of the first phase of development would be to only develop the core functionality.

A later phase would integrate the remaining functions. In this scenario, you essentially could have two projects. Therefore, clearly defining the project boundaries helps set the scope of work that is to be accomplished.

An example of a system boundary concept is:

The online store will integrate with the shopping cart and credit card purchasing modules for the initial release.

The second release will contain social media integration modules.

Project Risks

State the known risks. These risks are generally at a high-level since not much is known about the details of the project yet. If a Cost-Benefits Analysis was performed, then risks identified during the Cost Benefit Analysis should be placed here.

For example, if the project is going to span 5 years and touch multiple third party systems, then integration and technology change would be risks to consider.

Project Deliverables

Identify the products and services that the project will deliver. The intent of this section is to list the product or system deliverables and not the project management

Project Milestones

Identify the project milestones.

Note that these can still be used even if Agile is the methodology of choice, since the information is fairly general and it does not impose the specificity of the deliverables as you would in a full waterfall project schedule.

Rough Order of Magnitude (ROM) Estimate

Provide ROM estimate information here. If the work has been decomposed and a ROM estimate calculated, then provide the information here

Also, note that this can still be used for Agile, the difference is that the hours will simply not be used in a linear fashion as they are in a Waterfall project.

Activity	Estimated Time
Initiation	100-150 Resource Hours
Planning	100-200 Resource Hours
Development	200-400 Resource Hours
Testing	100-150 Resource Hours
Deployment	100-150 Resource Hours

The Planning Phase:

In a Waterfall methodology, the Planning phase is arguably the most important phase in the project.

A safe estimate would be that approximately 40% of the project manager's time would be spent in this area.

During the planning phase, the project is developed further and the details necessary for it to begin work are fleshed out. The Planning phase contains many key processes which we will list here:

- Develop Project Plan
- Scope Planning
- Scope Definition
- Create WBS
- Activity Definition
- Activity Sequencing
- Activity Resource Estimation
- Schedule Development
- Cost Estimating
- Cost Budgeting
- Quality Planning
- Human Resource Planning
- Communication planning
- Plan Contracting

The Project Plan:

The Project Plan is the key output of the PLANNING phase.

For a Waterfall project, this is the document that should be the big, huge document that contains all of the project detailed information, as opposed to the Project Charter, which should be briefer.

At a minimum, the Project Plan should contain the following information:

- An overview of the reasons for your project
- A detailed description of intended results
- A list of all constraints the project must address
- A list of all assumptions related to the project

- A list of all required work
- A breakdown of the roles you and your team members will play
- A detailed project schedule
- Needs for personnel, funds, and non-personnel resources (such as equipment, facilities, and information)
- A description of how you plan to manage any significant risks and uncertainties
- Plans for project communications
- Plans for ensuring project quality

Scope Definition:

Creating Project Scope is another major process within the Planning process group.

The Scope is the specific work that will be done in the project.

The Scope will be defined in a basic Scope statement, and either the work can proceed from there, or can be taken one step further and broken down into a Work Breakdown Structure (WBS).

Project Scope:

Project Scope is the definition of the actual work that is to be done for the project. Be sure to include and differentiate with specificity what is/is not included as part of the scope statement. Here is an example of the format of a Scope Statement:

Note: SEE APPENDIX 7 FOR A SAMPLE SCOPE STATEMENT

Obviously, for a large project, a significant amount of detail will need to be provided here. A specific degree of attention should be paid to the specific area as to what is NOT in scope.

Many times by including this, issues of "scope creep" can be avoided and conflicts anticipated ahead of time.

I have encountered the issue many times in which not having a specific item noted as specifically included, led to scope creep and unhappy stakeholders at the end of the project.

Don't let this happen, and put as much detail into the Scope Statement as possible.

Project Work Breakdown Structure (WBS)

If you have decomposed the high-level work that needs to be done, then provide the high-level work breakdown structure (WBS) here. A high-level WBS is sometimes referred to as a Rough Order of Magnitude WBS, or ROM WBS

The Work Breakdown Structure (WBS) is a simple list of tasks that need to be done at their most basic and tangible level.

Tasks in a WBS are organized into functional areas and expanded out until they reach a logical level of specificity such that they can be completed.

These tasks are then presented in the approximate order in which they must be completed, including each task's start and finish dates.

The WBS is a hierarchical chart that divides and decomposes work into more manageable components.

The WBS breaks down until we reach a level with tangible **Work Packages,** which is the component that can actually be scheduled and assigned.

The key function of the WBS is to enable these individual tasks to then be budgeted and planned.

The WBS helps accomplish the following:

- Enables more accurate estimating
- Enables cost estimating

- Helps stakeholders to visualize the project

WBS is all about identifying the work, not in the planning or scheduling of it.

Steps in building the WBS:

- Split teams into two groups
- Top-down group can assess the big picture – stakeholders and management
- Bottom-up thinkers such as the actual staff and developers can identify the actual specific tasks to be done.

Estimating Task and Project Time:

- Use a team to develop estimates
- This helps to identify and average our varying estimates

Task Estimation and Preventing Padded Estimates:

One issue that we commonly struggle with is the difference between task duration in hours to complete and then resource availability.

In other words, the task is assigned to one developer, scheduled for 40 hours worth of work. Logic will suggest to us that this goes on the schedule for one week, but the developer is only available 50% to our project.

When scheduling tasks, it is very important to factor in both task duration and availability and calculating accordingly.

We will take a brief sidebar here and point out that this factor is one of our many rationales for using Agile instead of waterfall because the idea is that the team is always 100% available for the duration of the sprint.

But in a waterfall methodology, use the following super simple formula to determine the full duration of a task based on your resource's planned availability.

Duration = Effort * (%Availability * 10)

The Execution Phase:

Project Execution is the phase in which the work actually gets done in the project.

In a Waterfall project, this means that all of the work will be completed, and then moved forward to the monitoring and controlling phase.

The major process of the Execution phase is the *DIRECT PROJECT EXECUTION* phase, which is simply the accomplishment of all of the work that has been defined in the Project Scope Statement.

For Agile, Scrum, and AgilePM2020 projects, execution and monitoring will be completed together as part of each two-week sprint.

Planning should already be done and completed in the Planning phase, but the sprint planning meeting is also there each sprint for any specific sub planning that needs to be done at the sprint level.

Back to the Execution phase: the primary outputs of the Execution phase are the following:

- Deliverables
- Change Requests
- Work Performance Information

Work Performance Information:

This is a function of the Project Manager, who must gather updated information from the team and provide updates where and when they are required, as noted in the Communication Plan.

Work Performance Information includes:

- Schedule Progress
- Deliverable Status
- Keeping track of scheduled activities
- Costs

- Resource utilization

With this information, the project manager will provide updates to the status reports via status update meetings, shared status reports or other methods.

Acquiring Project Team:

Another process of the Execution phase is the Acquiring Project Team process. For projects in which there are team members unavailable for some reason or another, or there is a question as to when certain team members will be available, a waterfall project is best.

As opposed to an Agile project, where the team has likely already been formed, a waterfall approach enables the team to be built later and also for individuals to work in different time slots and different locations. For many projects, this can work just fine. Some shops that have limited resources, or outsource so much that enough team members cannot work in the same location, then this is the best model to use.

Parkinson's Law:

One reason that we recommend projects handle tasks by teams is the phenomenon known as Parkinson's Law. I am sure that many of you have already encountered this, which simply states that the "*work will expand to fill the time available to it*"

Well yeah. We have seen this in action many times and can fully admit that we have done it ourselves. For this reason, this particular weakness in human nature, we recommend that even in a waterfall methodology when assigning tasks, tasks should be assigned to a team of at least 2 people (no such thing as a 1-person team, right?)

This way, with multiple people working on a task, they spur each other on and hopefully overachieve rather than fall victim to Parkinson's Law.

We are really not big fans of individuals working on tasks by themselves. We understand that it happens out of necessity sometimes, but should be done only in a limited manner.

What we want, whether it is waterfall, Agile or AgilePM2020 is to build a great team that works well together.

This may sound like unrealistic idealism, and while we respect and understand the challenges, we strongly suggest that without a solid team environment that projects are doomed to fail or underachieve.

In our opinion, no Project can succeed without a solid team, no matter how great the product is, no matter how great the service is, and no matter how great the Project Manager manages the project.

The Monitoring/Controlling Phase:

The Monitoring and Controlling phase involves many steps, all of which are related to managing and performance monitoring. The following processes are all included in the Monitoring and Controlling Phase:

- Monitor and Control project work
- Integrated change control
- Scope verification
- Scope control
- Schedule control
- Cost Control
- Perform Quality Control
- Manage Project Team
- Performance Reporting
- Manage Stakeholders
- Risk Monitoring and Control
- Contract Administration

Schedule Control:

This involves controlling changes to the project schedule. This process takes the schedule management plan and the schedule baseline as inputs, and provides the performance measurements and requested changes as its outputs.

Cost Control:

The objective here is to manage the budget and ensure that the pace of the project is not going to exceed the allocated budget.

We focus on this process because with this process we can actually apply some metrics that will help understand and convey to upper management the current costs, trends, and forecast of the total project cost.

Various methods can be applied to calculate and evaluate cost control:

Budget at Completion (BAC) – this is the project budget

Planned Value (PV) – amount of work scheduled compared to the amount budgeted

Actual Costs (AC) – actual costs of the completed tasks

Earned Value (EV) – planned costs of completed tasks (how much it should have cost)

Variances:

Variances are simply the deviation from the plan based on current progress.

A cost variance would mean that based on the pace of the project's completed tasks, and the budget allotted; the project budget will be exceeded by a certain number. This number can also be negative, but not too many people worry when projects come in under budget.

Schedule Variance is simply the calculation, based upon current pace, of the completion date of the project compared to the planned completion date.

Note: this is one of those key areas of communication that Project Managers must master. If a project has hit approximately the 33% or 50% completion point, we strongly recommend that this information is provided to all key stakeholders early.

We recommend this for a couple of reasons:

First, if a project has hit the 1/3 to 1/2 mark, as a Project Manager, you will likely know if this time can be made up or not. If it appears that the pace is consistent, there are no additional resources that can be added later or other means of mitigating this risk, then notify the stakeholders.

Doing this prevents an unnecessary surprise later, and also conveys to the stakeholders that you are being honest with them and also proactive.

The second reason this is important is that it communicates the fact that certain features might cost more than expected and take longer than expected, which might mean the stakeholders **elect not to include them.**

I always make the case the Scope is the most flexible of the triple constraint items of Time, Cost, and Scope. Make these projections known to the stakeholders so they can really evaluate if the functionality is needed or not. You may be able to reduce the scope of the project this way.

Most people are reasonable when they are presented the facts in regards to cost, time and scope. They might initially rant and rave, but ultimately, most people have reasonable expectations.

Most of the time.

Variance Calculations

To calculate variances, you first need to calculate some key values and then apply some formulas.

Percentage Complete – this can be elusive, but at a simple level, this defines how much of the scheduled work has been completed.

Planned Value – Based on the percentage complete, how much of the budget should have been spent

Actual Cost – actual costs incurred on the project

Earned Value – we have the formula for earned value below, but basically, it states the amount of budget that should have been used based on the amount of work done. This is essentially a **ratio** of work completed to work budgeted.

With these three basic definitions, we can now move on to some formulas and then explain how best to use these for stakeholder updates.

The most important, in my mind, are Cost Variance and Schedule Variance. Here are three formulas that can be used for defining variances

Earned Value	Percent Complete * Budget at Completion	Example: 40% complete * (200000 budget) = 80,000 EV
Cost Variance	Earned Value – Actual Costs	EV = 80,000 – AC (100,000) = 20000 CV
Schedule Variance	Earned Value – Planned Value	EV = 80000 – PV 80000 = 0

Based on the calculations above, the sample project is 20,000 over projections, so based on pace it would end the project 20,000 over or more. On the other hand, there is no schedule variance, so the project is on time and on schedule.

Other Mechanisms to Calculate Earned Value:

We prefer the calculation noted above, but there are additional mechanisms that can be used to calculate Earned value such as

Weighted Milestones – milestones are assigned a budget value and the earned value is a comparison of milestones completed and total budget.

Quality Control Tools:

During the monitoring and controlling phase, the project manager takes on the role of an amateur statistician and uses a variety of tools to analyze the progress of the project.

Effective tools that can be used to analyze the health of projects include the following.

- Scatter Diagrams
- Run Chart
- Flow Chart
- Control Chart
- Cause and Effect Diagram
- Pareto Chart
- Histogram

All of these tools can be very effective in root cause analysis and other mechanisms of analysis. As an experienced project manager, I can honestly admit that it was not until I was taking my Lean Six Sigma training that I came to appreciate how useful these tools could be.

Seeing solid examples of each, I have subsequently used these to great success both in new projects and also to diagnose production issues and root cause analysis in production support.

Of all of the various quality control tools, we prefer two of them the most and will discuss and provide examples here.

Control Chart:

The Control Chart is a graphical display meant to note the results of a process over time.

The primary objective of a Control Chart is to indicate which consistent causes may indicate a true pattern, and eliminating outliers that exist.

Control charts may also be used to determine whether cost variances or schedule variances are outside of acceptable limits. As noted above, this analysis could be combined with the cost variance and schedule variance to perhaps explain the variances and prevent a projected variance from becoming a true overrun.

What are the primary purposes of Control Charts? The primary purpose of control charts is to determine if the process being reviewed has changed due to common causes or special causes.

Control charts can signal an out of control condition, which would indicate that a special cause of variation is present.

Types of Data Used For a Control Chart:

Continuous or Variable Data

- Measured on a scaled that can be infinitely divided
- *Examples: Length, Height, Weight, Time*

Discrete or Attribute Data:

- Examples: Counts, Binary Data, Nominal Data, Ordinal Data

Cause and Effect Diagram:

Also known as a Fishbone or Ishikawa Diagram, this involves determining how various issues can cause certain problems.

The idea of this is to gain root cause analysis through the identification and vetting of all potential causes, no matter how significant they may appear.

Manage Stakeholders:

The final monitoring and controlling phase that we will discuss is the Manage Stakeholders phase. Regardless of Project Management methodology, this is the key process within the Monitoring and Controlling phase

This process is all about Communication. This is repeated over and over throughout this book, so get used to it. The primary objectives in this process are to **proactively** deal with stakeholder concerns.

We say proactively, because if a concern becomes strong enough, then valid or not it becomes a problem for the Project Manager.

The Project Manager is responsible for all communication in the Waterfall model. In the Agile model it is split up a little bit more, but not so in Waterfall.

For communication, we discuss it more at length in a later chapter, but for now just want to recommend a certain strategy and combination of communication methods.

The first point is to *know your audience*. Do not just send a basic email to a key stakeholder. For upper management, so-called C-Level management, then yes an email, more formalized document is best.

For the key stakeholder, who is very involved in the project, multiple communication methods need to be implemented such as email, in-person, instant message/chat, conference calls, direct phone calls.

The Manage Stakeholders process is one in which the Project Manager again gets to play Psychologist. By playing psychologist, the PM must use their ability to read people and analyze and anticipate.

It is not always easy, but we highly recommend several informal meetings with key stakeholders to get a "read" or a sense of how they will be on a project and what their communication needs will be. A few conversations at the beginning of the project will save you a great deal of pain later.

One of our project managers had a project in place in which a key plant manager would be affected, and was not notified until the project went live.

Once this person learned of this, they went irate and made life difficult for the others on the team, solely because of the slight of not being included in the process all along.

Had the PM done their homework and known the personality that they were dealing with, it's very likely that this could have been avoided.

On the other hand, sometimes people are just *jackasses*.

Now, at this point, we have completed the planning, done all of the work, and monitoring and corrected our code and deployed to production.

All that is left now is to CLOSE the project

Closure:

The Closing phase is, you guessed it, the phase in which the project is formally closed.

This marks the end for the waterfall process.

The Closing phase consists of two primary processes:

- Contract Closure
- Close Project

Contract Closure:

The contract closure process is the process for completing each contract, including the resolution of any open items, and closing all contracts.

Contract Closure involves Product Verification and Administrative Closure as sub-processes.

Lessons Learned/ Vendor Review:

This is the opportunity to note any serious issues encountered with the vendor. Any ideas for process improvements, recommendations, etc should be noted here.

Close Project:

The Close Project process is the major process of the CLOSING phase.

The Close Project process is when the Project Manager documents and finalizes all activities to gain formal project acceptance by the sponsor.

Essentially, this is when the Project Manager gets sign-off for the project. This is something one might assume is automatic, but some sponsors have been known to hold up on signing off or refuse to sign off altogether for a myriad of reasons.

This is should be addressed in planning, once the criteria for project success has been established and met, then sign-off should follow with no objections.

The Close Project process consists of two sub-processes: Contract Closure and Administrative Closure.

We have already discussed Contract Closure, so now let's look at Administrative Closure.

The primary functions of the Administrative Closure subprocess is to transfer the project product or services to production and/or operations.

This includes the key steps of archiving project records, analyzing project success/failures and gathering lessons learned as noted earlier.

Another key factor in the Close Project process is Release Resources, in which we set the project team free to roam in the wild....or at least until we need them for the next project.

Waterfall Summary:

For a Waterfall project, it is very important that the phases be followed very consistently. Documentation is going to be more involved for a waterfall project than an Agile project. The Planning, Execution, and Monitoring/Controlling phases will be the most involved, with planning likely being the most work for the Project Manager.

Good candidates for Waterfall projects are projects with team members in different locations, schedule conflicts, or infrastructure projects.

Also, for projects in which the scope is fully known, Waterfall could be the best bet. Software projects rarely have this luxury, but say there is an implementation project in which a third party software is to be installed on one machine, there is no customization required, then waterfall could work.

Now that we have covered the wonders of Waterfall, let's discuss Agile for a bit and then on to Agile PM 2020.

But first, let's review how the topics discussed in this chapter impact our Case Study:

CASE STUDY:

True Spirit Software and Energy Corporation

The waterfall methodology will most likely need to be maintained for several of the in-progress projects.

Even for some of the newer projects, the internal audit department will continue to review that basic project management documents are maintained and updated.

For this reason, Richard has decided to continue to use traditional Project Managers for all project planning, structure and audit documentation requirements.

Not being all that familiar with the personnel needs of Agile projects, he has decided to defer this decision on additional staffing requirements until they have more information about the specific projects.

So, Richard informs the CIO Patty that Bill and Mark will be used for the existing projects, and new projects that are fairly straightforward. Bill and Mark will be the primary initiation points for all new projects and be charged with creating all project charters and maintaining all of the audit information.

Mark views this as an increase in his authority, but Richard has to have the awkward conversation with Mark to tell him that this change is actually a reduction in the role of the traditional Project Manager.

Mark argues this point, but the ultimate answer and opinion is that of the CIO, so although he rants and protests, at first, Mark soon recognizes the true reality of the situation and learns to accommodate it.

Richard also has a counseling session with Steve to tell him about the new roles for everyone and expresses his concern that Steve can adapt to the new requirements and new Project Management landscape.

Steve agrees with these concerns, and after an hour-long discussion, it is determined that Steve will go to PMI-ACP training as a part of his annual professional development efforts. As an already credentialed Project Management Professional (PMP), this will help him to maintain his credential by providing over 30 PDU credits.

Steve is still not convinced about Agile, and while he pretends to go along to please his manager, internally he is seething.

Richard is pleased with the manner in which these PMs responded to the changes but still fears that the CIO ultimately may want to replace all Project Managers with Scrum Masters, a move that he vehemently opposes.

As a proactive move, Richard plans to make Certified Scrum Master courses available to all those who request it.

Richard, at this point believes that all is proceeding well with the adoption of agile, but there are many forces that are resistant to the change, and Steve is one of the most impactful.

In his next project status meeting with VP of Energy Trading, Jim Ballenger, Steve has a few words to add in regards to this new Agile project management methodology.

"Hey Jim," Steve says, "have you heard about the changes to our project management approach that we are implementing this year?'

"Just rumors really, I haven't heard anything official yet," Ballenger responds. "Something called 'Agile' but I must admit that I don't know much about it."

Steve shakes his head and doesn't respond.

Now, Ballenger becomes concerned based upon Steve's body language.

"Why? How is this going to affect us? I assume negatively based on your reaction." Ballenger asks.

Steve continues to shake his head.

"Not entirely sure." Steve says, "But all I know is that whenever there are changes of this magnitude it always seems to slow things down around here."

Ballenger looks concerned, and then an angry look develops on his face.

"Just let me handle this." Ballenger says. "I can put a stop to it."

Steve smiles. His first step at sabotaging the Agile change is already in progress.

CHAPTER 4: Agile Software Development

"Nothing is less productive than to make more efficient what should not be done at all."
-Peter Drucker

What in the world is Agile Software Development?

Agile Software development refers to the process of iterative development. The primary ideas behind it appear to be rooted in common sense as the focus is on working software and customer satisfaction as opposed to a thorough planning phase and extensive documentation.

The quote above relates to Agile because Agile projects will ultimately identify scope items that are less important, and towards the end of the project many of these items will not be completed. Therefore, the inefficiencies of developing unnecessary items will be avoided.

Agile is actually an umbrella term that refers to iterative and incremental software development methodologies that include the following:

- Scrum
- KANBAN
- Extreme Programming
- Lean
- Feature-Driven Development(FDD)

To quote the Agile manifesto: "We have come to value:

- Individuals and Interactions over Processes and Tools
- Working Software over Comprehensive Documentation
- Customer Collaboration over Contract Negotiation
- Responding To Change over Following a plan"

Please visit the Agile Manifesto web site for the full set of principles for the Agile approach at www.Agilemanifesto.org

In our analysis of the four key points listed on the manifesto, we note that all four really are about two key things at the center of it:

- More involved customers and team members
- Working software that contains those items that are important now as opposed to what may have been important six months ago

Of all the major points of the Agile manifesto the point that we stress the most is the final point: "responding to change over following a plan"

Yes, yes and yes.

With software development, the likelihood of having all of the functionality addressed, designed and planned right away is very low. As the product begins to take shape, other ideas are formed and opinions changed.

Webster defines *Agile* as being:

- Able to move quickly and easily
- Quick, smart and clever

We do something as lame as providing a definition just to get a point to hit home. We feel that Agile is the definition of being quick, smart and clever in regards to software development.

In our experience, we have learned that right or not, the customer IS always right. Going along with that, we have identified that the customer usually doesn't really know what they want.

There are likely two major ways that this can be handled and with Agile the less confrontational approach can be taken. Take the example of the project sponsor who insists that a web site should have ten total web pages, but you realize that three of them have duplicate functionality of three other pages.

As the project manager, you point this out to the sponsor. The objection is noted, but the sponsor still stubbornly insists that the web site have ten pages.

I have worked with several Project Managers who would not let this point go. They would argue tooth and nail with the project sponsor that this site should only have six or seven pages, and almost **insist** upon it.

We feel that we would rather avoid that career limiting move. Sometimes people cannot be talked out of their position, and in our case that is just fine.

With Agile, you can build the project plan out in such a way that the sprints are managed to focus on the key functionality first and then phase everything else in later.

With Agile, you can **demonstrate** to the sponsor why the functionality is covered with the core seven web pages, and illustrate why the other three pages are not needed. Then point out that if those pages are to be added, then other items cannot be done.

It is not recommended to defy the sponsor, simply guide them in the direction of selecting another alternative that makes more sense.

In this book, when we refer to Agile we will be referring almost always to Scrum and the Scrum processes. There are other types of Agile such as KANBAN and Extreme programming, but we are more familiar, and therefore comfortable, with the Scrum methodologies.

Scrum and KANBAN:

Scrum is a well-defined process framework. The introduction of Scrum is quite a change for a team not used to Agile development at all. The steep learning curve involves the following:

- Working in iterations
- Building cross-functional teams
- Appoint a product owner
- Appoint a Scrum master

KANBAN is not structured. It is more of a process of organizing all work on a KANBAN board, where each work item has states that it passes through during the entire process:

- In Progress
- Testing
- Ready for Release
- Release

In KANBAN, there are generally multiple swim lanes or pipelines all running simultaneously.

In general, Scrum and KANBAN are both specfic shapings of an Agile software methodology.

So, which to use, Scrum or KANBAN?

We believe that for a new implementation of Agile into your enterprise, Scrum is the way to go. Scrum is more beneficial is there is a need to improve process efficiency. This is typically the case when organizations seek to implement Agile.

If, on the other hand, the processes are already efficient, but merely need a few tweaks, then it might be wise to consider KANBAN.

The Core of the Scrum Process:

Scrum at its most simplistic could be defined as an iterative, incremental project skeleton.

Imagine Scrum as two circles, in which the lower circle represents an iteration of development that occurs sequentially. The second circle, the upper circle, will represent the daily inspection that occurs during the iteration. During this inspection the individual team members will meet and inspect the activities and then make the necessary changes.

This image gives a very high-level idea of the Scrum process. We will discuss the specifics of

At its core, Scrum is a simple set of roles, responsibilities and meetings that are constant. By removing unnecessary unpredictability, more time can be focused on those facets of the project that cannot be predicted.

To explore what Scrum is and how it operates we will discuss in order the following:

- Overall Scrum Process
- Scrum Meetings
- Scrum Roles
- Scrum Documentation/Artifacts

The Scrum Iteration Process or Sprint:

At an extremely high-level, a Scrum iteration process which we call a **sprint** follows these steps:

1. The team reviews the items that it must do
2. The team selects what they all agree can be completed within this sprint
3. The team proceeds in its efforts to complete the selected tasks
4. The completed product is delivered for review by the product owner
5. All items not completed in this sprint are put back on the board to be scheduled in a later sprint

Scrum Meetings and Specifics of the Scrum Process:

During the ongoing Scrum process, there are three main types of meetings that occur for each Sprint during the project.

These three meetings are as follows:

- Sprint Planning Meeting
- Sprint Review Meeting
- Sprint Retrospective

Sprint Planning Meeting:

At the beginning of every sprint, the Product Owner leads a meeting in which they present the top items on the product backlog to the team.

The Scrum team selects the work that they feel that can be completed during the duration of the sprint. This work is then moved to the **Sprint Backlog** to be worked during the current sprint.

The Sprint Backlog is simply the list of items selected to be worked for this sprint only. This should not be confused with the Product Backlog, which is the list of work items for the entire project.

Sprint Review Meeting:

At the end of the sprint, the team demonstrates the completed tasks as a group. This is typically done with the Product owner and stakeholders, who can, at this point, either approve or not approve the tasks as completed.

Sprint Retrospective:

The Sprint Retrospective can be done in parallel with the Sprint Review meeting, but it is intended to be for the Scrum team only. This is the opportunity for the team to self-critique and evaluate what has been working and what has not been working.

I introduce the concept of floating-rotating teams later, but this would be an opportunity to consider modifying the team for the next sprint based on performance or other concerns.

Scrum Role Definitions:

We view Scrum and Agile Project Management 2020 as having three key roles of project leadership and then a strong team.

Our key three leadership roles are the:

- Scrum Master
- Product Owner
- Project Manager

Scrum features roles that are a little bit different from those roles of traditional Project Management (Waterfall).

In Scrum, for example, there is no obvious role for the traditional Project Manager. There are two roles that can be mapped from that of a traditional project manager, but there is not strictly a Project Manager-only role.

Instead the role of the Project Manager is split into two roles which could be performed by a traditional project manager if this person has technical skills (Scrum Master) or business skills/knowledge (Product Owner).

Now that this has been introduced, let's look at the specific roles in Scrum and discuss their specific responsibilities.

Product Owner

This person is responsible for representing the stakeholders and the business to the development team. The product owner should be a person with vision, authority and availability. In this way, the product owner should almost be someone on the business side or a very strong business analyst who knows the business extremely well.

Product owners need not be involved in the day to day operations of the team, but should be available each day to provide advice should it be needed. Although a business analyst or traditional project manager could fill this role, we have seen it work best when the Product Owner is from the business side.

The Product Owner will be making key decisions about prioritization and task selection for the sprints, so it benefits the team greatly if the Product Owner is not from within IT, but from the business side.

Scrum Master

The Scrum Master is responsible for ensuring that Scrum practices are followed by everyone. The Scrum Master also acts as a facilitator between the Product Owner and the team. Note here that despite the seemingly commanding term of Master, the Scrum Master does **not** actually manage the team.

This is one reason that traditional project managers might struggle if taking this role. The role might be more suitable to a **technical lead**, which has good leadership skills but also shows interest in moving into management.

The Team

This self managing unit is responsible for self organizing to complete work. This development team contains approximately seven fully dedicated members, preferably co-located and in a location protected from outside distractions.

A typical team would include a mix of software engineers, architects, developers, database analysts (DBAs), testers and QA experts. A key point here is that the team has the autonomy and responsibility to meet the goals of the sprint.

Project Manager

This role is NOT explicitly listed as a role in Scrum, but we are listing it here anyway. In our opinion, whether they are called Program Managers, Portfolio Managers or PMO Managers, there are still some responsibilities that a project manager is better suited for.

In AgilePM2020, a project manager will work **with** the product owner and Scrum master to define the parameters of the project. Initial project documentation should still be completed, such as a Project Charter, Risk and Issues Log, etc.

This should all proceed as normal and this is the Project Manager's responsibility to complete.

There will be differences, of course, such as the Project Plan would morph into a Sprint Plan, and other documents would not be as extensive as you would have in a Waterfall project.

So, for the Initiation and Planning phases, the Project Manager role is important. For the Execution and Quality Control phase, the project manager's responsibilities are a little different, and can be split between the Product Owner and the Scrum Master.

David B. Twilley, PMP, CSM

Scrum: Multiple Options for How to Use Project Managers

If a company chose to do this, by removing the Project Manager from the Execution facet of the project, a Project Manager could focus their time and energy towards the initiation and planning phases of that many more projects.

This would likely increase their project management bandwidth by 50%, since now they only have to focus on half as much of the project process as they did before.

The potential downside to this becomes the fact that the Project Manager turns over the execution of the project to the Product Owner and Scrum Master, so then there is the question of who is ultimately responsible for its success or failure.

This is a grey area and is one reason that we recommend that the Project Manager stay involved in one facet or another.

We still believe that the Product Owner should be either the sponsor or the key stakeholder, who is invested enough and has the authority on the business side to get things done.

Also, we don't believe that non-technical Project Managers should be Scrum Masters since they lack the knowledge to contribute anything significant to the team's work. These individuals would likely be better served as Program or Portfolio managers.

Technical Project Managers could take on the role of Scrum Master, if the size of the team mandated this, but otherwise keep them in their role as Project Manager if possible.

Agile Project Documentation:
Product Backlog:

The Product Backlog is essentially the scope of the project broken down into manageable units of work or User Stories.

This product backlog is the master scope list from which the Scrum team and product owner identify and select the work efforts that will compose each sprint.

The Product Backlog is a dynamic, evolving document. It should never be viewed as a completed document, nor should all of the items that comprise it be viewed as mandatory.

Items can be added at any time here, because just because they are added to the Product Backlog does not mean that they are going to be worked.

This requires the Product Owner to prioritize and the Product Owner, Scrum Master and the team to add the item to the Sprint Backlog.

Until this happens, an item could theoretically remain on the Product Backlog indefinitely and never be worked.

The **Product Owner** is responsible for the contents and the prioritization of the Product Backlog.

This is yet another reason why it is better for the Product Owner to be either from the business or very deeply connected to the business. The Product Owner will be the primary driver of the priorities on the Product Backlog, and they need to be representing the business well or this could backfire later on.

The Sprint Backlog:

The Sprint Backlog can be thought of as the current Sprint task list. These are the items that the Product Owner requests be completed during the sprint, and that the Scrum Master and team commit to work during the specific sprint.

Again, to visit our original document, here is an example of the Agile Scrum cycle, which clearly indicates the key areas:

As you can see the process starts here with the Product Backlog. The list of papers, sticky notes, or whatever mechanism used to create your list

Next in the Sprint Planning meeting, the product backlog items selected to be worked are added to the Sprint Backlog to be worked during the current sprint.

And the sprint iterations are the two week sessions during which the sprint backlog items are worked and then put into the position where they are considered "potentially shippable".

This means that it may not necessarily go live at the end of these two weeks, but it would be ready to go if need be.

Why Not Release the Product Every Two Weeks?

This comes back to the idea that each project needs to be managed as its own entity. Sure, a two week release is ideal in the sprint and Scrum environments. There are several shops however, that only approves releases once per month, or has some other limited schedule that precludes a strict following of this two-week paradigm.

Users also do not have the schedule availability to enable enough full UAT to accommodate the two-week sprints. Trust me, as long as the development team is completing the work and preparing the code for deployment, it really is of secondary concern if the team actually deploys to production.

This is where the relationship of the Product Owner is of paramount importance. The Product Owner could want out-of-cycle releases, perhaps occasionally insist upon it, or by working as a partner with the IT department understand the need to deploy during the release window made available by the IT team.

Agile Project Estimation:

This is one of the areas in which Agile immediately deviates from the Waterfall model. Instead of a Project Manager either building the estimate by themselves, or perhaps working with one developer or one other person on estimates, Scrum involves the entire team.

Task estimation is done with the Product Owner, The Scrum Master and the entire team together as a part of the sprint planning meeting.

I have to again point out how much more effective this is than the Waterfall method of scheduling, and I will site a specific example to back up that claim:

One of my colleagues was a non-technical project manager. He worked with two developers who understood that he was not technical, so they provided him padded estimates. Not being technical, he was unable to challenge these estimates. Also, the developers, without any peers or supervisors to challenge their estimates, were free to pad them without any professional guilt.

Sometimes these can be innocent mistakes, but sometimes people are taking advantage of you. Scrum and Agile helps to mitigate this risk of time padding by putting the estimation in the hands of the entire team.

Time Estimation in Scrum:

In a Scrum/Agile environment, one of our recommendations for task estimation is the technique known as "Planning Poker".

Planning Poker involves a mechanism by which each member of the team helps to set the estimate for each task, as we mentioned earlier.

Planning Poker, which was created by James Grenning, but largely popularized by Mike Cohn in his book ***Agile Estimating and Planning***, is a technique that focuses on estimating tasks in terms of **relative effort.**

Rather than to define tasks in terms of hours, they are instead defined in relative size. It is consensus based, and in our opinion a greate mechanism for developing good estimates.

One reason for this is the effect of groups on tightening the estimates. It is far less likely to have exaggerated or padded estimates since several individuals are contributing to the estimates. When one or maybe two individuals have to do the estimating on their own, I have seen a far greater propensity to embellish or pad.

Planning Poker utilizes the following story point values as a starting point:

0	½	1	2	3	5
8	13	20	40	100	?

Planning Poker utilizes an estimation technique in which PBIs are estimated in the terms of "Story Points". These story points do not naturally correlate to hours, work days or any other metric.

The story points are rated with numbers, which correspond to effort, such as 1, 2, 3, 5, 8 and higher. These numbers roughly correspond to the Fibonacci sequence of numbers. Now, this is not a topic for this book to cover, but the Fibonacci sequence is quite fascinating and bears further investigation.

Comparative Analysis:

Whereas estimating a task effort by itself could be difficult, it's that much easier to compare tasks to **each other**. A team may not know how much effort that web page will take to finish, but they know it won't take as long as that stock trading algorithm.

By comparing items in terms of relative effort, it becomes easier to quantify and tighten these estimates.

Team Pressure:

This is one of our favorite reasons. Speaking from personal experience as a former developer, I will let you in on a little secret: *all developers pad their estimates.* I know, I know, quite shocking but very true.

In my experience, this is done for two reasons:

- Rounding, vague estimates
- Fear of reprisal
- Competing priorities

So what we mean by this is that developers round up, way up when providing estimates instead of taking much time to get an accurate number.

The second reason, fear of reprisal, is simple. By holding the responsibility by themselves, the developer feels the need to pad a little to not miss the deadline, thereby getting in potential trouble. It also doesn't help when micro-managing Project Managers come by their desk every day or more often to get frequent updates. It could be argued that this very cycle leads to the padded estimates. The Project Manager should share some blame in this game.

And finally, the issue of competing priorities is crucial. Say the developer provided the estimate in May and their schedule was wide open, so sure they should be able to complete that task in two weeks in June.

As June arrives, this same developer suddenly is on two other projects each of which consumes about 10 hours of his week. Suddenly, his original estimate is completely askew. Is this because he provided a poor estimate, or a simple casualty of working on multiple projects?

So with the entire team estimating tasks together, and with the team being dedicated to the project for the duration of the sprint, estimates are going to be far more accurate.

This is not to imply that they will always be perfect, but they are better than the traditional Project Manager or Developer estimation.

Iterative Process- "Practice Makes Perfect"

A final benefit of this Planning Poker approach is that with a cycle of "estimate, work, deploy, estimate, work, deploy" the entire process becomes more accurate as the sprints evolve.

The more often the teams complete the estimation cycle, the better and more accurate these estimates become. It becomes a skill that the team develops.

Note again, that these numbers do **not** correspond to units of time and should not be viewed in such a manner. This is one additional reason that traditional project managers would be somewhat lost in a Scrum or AgilePM2020 environment.

I have worked with many such individuals who just have to convert story points into something that they can put on their Gantt charts, and that is simply not the purpose.

No, story points are designed to serve as a cumulative total that provides the team a rough idea how much effort they can take on for each sprint. In the early going, it will be difficult to determine this rate, also known as **Velocity**.

What is VELOCITY?

Velocity is simply the number of story points completed in the sprint.

For an individual sprint it is less important, but as a cumulative factor across multiple sprints, it is effective to establish a baseline goal for a number of story points to target for each sprint.

Like most other facets of Agile, Velocity is something that will get more and more accurate as the sprints move forward, and also as the team learns to work together.

Once a few sprints have been completed, it will be established that the team can successfully complete 25-30 points per sprint (just an example) and each subsequent sprint will use this as a baseline. As efficiencies improve, this number could potential move up but at least there is an initial baseline with which to work.

Burndown Chart:

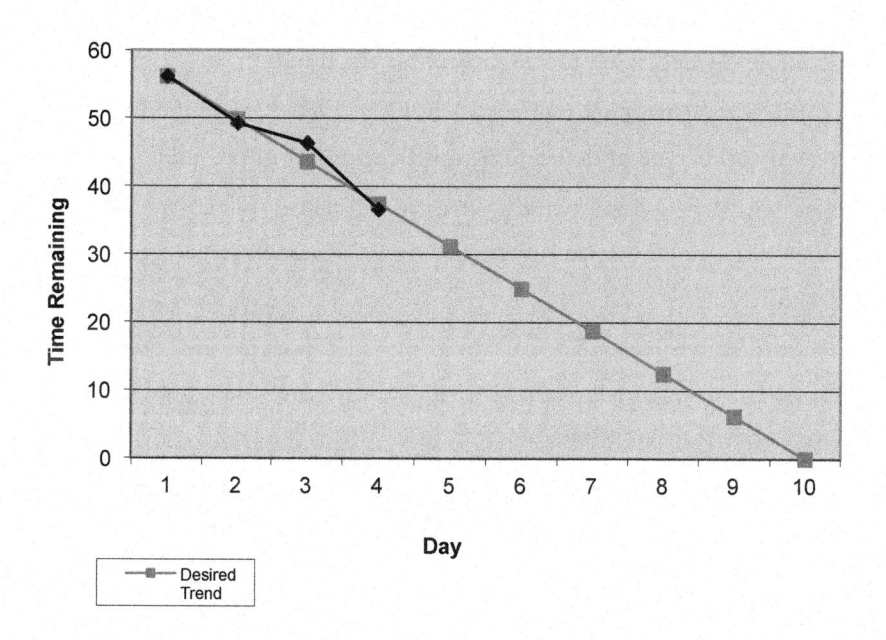

A **Burndown Chart** is simply a graphical representation of work left to do versus time. The remaining work is put on the vertical axis, with the time displaying on the horizontal. As an analytical tool, it is very useful for predicting when all of the work will be completed.

Agile Project management follows a circular, iterative pattern as noted before. Once the execution of the project starts, the sprint iterations become the focus of the project, and they continue until the entire set of task items have been completed, or at least enough have been completed to satisfy the customer.

This consistent plan, select, code and test cycles are beneficial in that constant progress is being made and that tangible benefits can be demonstrated early and often to the stakeholders.

Limitations of Agile and Scrum:

We are actually big proponents of Agile and Scrum but we do recognize issues and potential problems with Scrum. For one, a truly Agile team is one that is completely dedicated to the project for the duration.

In our current environment of multi-tasking and cross-functional matrix environments, this type of dedication is difficult if not impossible.

Secondly, while the close working nature of teams is mostly beneficial, sometimes this can be distracting during times where extreme concentration is necessary.

For this reason, we have seen certain companies have rooms called "think rooms" where individuals can go to concentrate and get something completed away from multiple distractions.

We like the idea of these "think rooms" outside of the main project team area for the occasional need to work solo for short periods of time.

Flexible Teams:

For this reason, one of the adjustments that we make to clients is that they maintain a core team of 7 people, along with an additional 2-3 that can be rotated in occasionally.

This way in times in which a team member is needed elsewhere, they can take a sprint or two off and we can rotate others in to take their place.

Very commonly, developers support multiple users, project initiatives and business units and this time away from the project enables them to address and support these other groups.

Also, build in a plan to accommodate team member's vacations and time off and do what can be realistically done in the planning phase to plan sprints accordingly using this schedule of availability.

The makeup of a team should feature a combination of developers, analysts, QA people, and other specialists. When building a team, the type of tasks to complete should lead you to develop a good staffing plan.

The Product Owner and Scrum Master should have a good idea of the type of team that they need way before the first sprint begins.

For those roles in which the majority of the effort will reside, have at least two of that type of role staffed on the project, and expect that multiple team members with that skill will be on every sprint.

The more specialized roles, with fewer tasks should have one member on the team and maybe one backup, but you can likely get away without one. For most development projects, for example, you would ideally want about four on every sprint, and then one in reserve to rotate in.

An Example of 2 Sprints using a rotating team of 10 people

SPRINT 1

Name	Team Role	Active/Inactive
Jamie	Developer	Active
Bruce	Developer	Active
Nitil	Developer	Active
James	Scrum Master	Active
DeSean	Business Analyst	Active
Brenda	Developer	Active
Rahul	QA	Active
Shauna	Developer	Inactive
Juan	QA	Inactive
Neha	Business Analyst	Inactive

SPRINT 2

Name	Team Role	Active/Inactive
Jamie	Developer	Inactive
Bruce	Developer	Active
Nitil	Developer	Active
James	Scrum Master	Active
DeSean	Business Analyst	Inactive
Brenda	Developer	Active
Rahul	QA	Inactive
Shauna	Developer	Active
Juan	QA	Active
Neha	Business Analyst	Active

So, what we have done here is simply rotate a few folks out each sprint thereby providing them some time to focus on other projects. This might be especially useful in situations in which you only need one of a certain type of skill, such as a DBA, QA or an Architect.

Or, another alternative is to attempt to group all of these tasks into one or two sprints and then have all of these specialists assigned to those sprints to be able to focus and complete all of their more specialized tasks.

Agile and Lean Concepts:

Several concepts in the LEAN philosophy focus on the elimination of waste. Many of these Lean concepts are very similar to the ideas of Agile and AgilePM2020.

Our focus and that of many other Agile strategies is to keep it simple, focus on only the work that needs to be done, when it needs to be done.

The 8 Wastes

Lean defines the 8 wastes as the following:

- Waiting
- Overproduction
- Over processing
- Transportation
- Inventory
- Motion
- Defects
- Skills

Admittedly, some of these do not directly correlate to software development, but many of them do.

Waiting – this is defined as people waiting on others, information, product, or machines.

In Agile, this is eliminated as part of its core focus. With Agile, the team is working together, no one person can serve as a bottleneck and create inefficiencies with people sitting idly by waiting for their step in the process.

I worked in a large IT shop for over a year and a half, and each Wednesday all of the Project Managers, Business Analysts, and Management met to go over all projects and work streams. It was a waterfall shop, with a very functional matrix.

As people gave their project updates and we went around the room, if I counted the number of times someone said "waiting on…." it would easily be in the double figures. Week after week, person after person would say they were at an impasse because they were waiting on someone else before they could do their work, therefore no updates.

These individuals were basically passing the buck and not taking ownership for their own tasks, not very impressive.

How efficient is that?

Overproduction – this is defined as producing too much, too soon. There is no direct correlation to software, except that with Agile the focus is completing only as much as is needed when it is needed.

Over-Processing – defined as doing more than the customer is willing to pay for.

This is a definite correlation to Agile and one of its key benefits. By completing development in an iterative fashion, we eliminate any unneeded items.

Transportation – defined as the movement of people or things. No real correlation to software development

Inventory – defined as the buildup of paperwork, material, supplies, etc. There is no real correlation to software development.

Defects – Defined as the suppliers or analysts providing incomplete or incorrect information.

This is definitely correlated to Agile, as with Agile we have the short two week sprints, so if there are issues they will still be there, but will be caught much more quickly than defects or requirement mistakes would be caught in a Waterfall environment.

Closing Argument on Agile:

It is probably obvious based on the tone of the book that we prefer an Agile approach for software development. This is mostly true because of our experience in the industry and the observation that most requirements are never really well defined.

What I mean by this is the simple fact that most customers or stakeholders are not completely sure what they want until they start looking at it. Sure, they have the basic concept, but as it gets fleshed out they realize little by little exactly how they want it to look.

By taking an Agile strategy it is as if the team helps the stakeholders realize their vision, keeps them engaged in the entire process, and enables them to change their minds with minimal impact.

Probably the biggest reason that we prefer Agile as a rule is the focus on the team. We really like the team-first approach to development for many reasons.

We think developers are more productive this way, they don't need a Project Manager looking over their shoulders every day or requiring daily updates. We like the idea of a technical lead getting some additional responsibility and completing the role of Scrum Master with some appropriate training. We like the team doing the task estimation as a group rather than individually with the Project Manager.

When is Agile not appropriate?

Again, one of our key points in this book is that one should not be solely an Agile or Waterfall evangelist. Instead look for the correct situation and react accordingly.

For this reason, Agile may not be appropriate because of your client, because of your sponsor or the specific needs of the project. We are of the opinion that software implementation (that is the purchase and installation of third party software solutions) are not suitable for Agile.

Nor do we believe that infrastructure projects, those involving the coordination of server upgrades, increasing capacity, ordering hardware, etc.

This should all be considered when evaluating the needs of the project. In our opinion, Agile is the most beneficial for custom software development and Infrastructure and Third party software installations work best with a Waterfall approach.

Our recommendation: Proceed Slowly:

What we mean is that the business needs to be handled and led into this new methodology slowly, and also they need to be continually sold on it as you proceed. Let them know that there are certain issues that will be encountered, and then do what you can to anticipate and mitigate these problems before they occur.

Here are some warnings for possible pushback and resistance that can result from an enterprise change to Agile.

Major Problems with Agile:

1. Agile Reveals problems that were hidden
    a. Long-established processes that have been well integrated meet with bureaucratic resistance to change
    b. People don't care for the harsh truths
2. Agile Creates transparency
    a. Transparency leads to revolt and people tend to give up on the process because of initial difficulties
3. Agile demands fixing root causes
    a. Unfortunately, sometimes the business does not want to deal with it.
    b. Reveals the fact that there have been certain cultural limitations, which makes certain people defensive.

So, in conclusion, we advise that a realistic approach is taken when moving to an Agile methodology, do not press or push the business too quickly, nor expect them to fully embrace the concept right away.

As an IT department, we must serve the needs of the business and the customer(as painful as that may be sometimes).

It is best to not push them too quickly or else you risk a pushback and any progress made moving towards Agile may otherwise be lost.

CASE STUDY:

True Spirit Software and Energy Corporation

Richard already has plans for the first Agile project.

Bill, the Project Manager who is a PMI-ACP and has a fairly agreeable personality will manage the first agile project for the company.

Richard will start with one fairly low profile project which is sponsored by a business manager that Richard has an especially close relationship with.

He has his Project Manager in place, but he will now need to identify the Scrum Master and the Product Owner if this project will be appropriately staffed.

Bill has recommended that they consider Bhaskal, who has been a technical lead for about five years. Not only is Bhaskal technically proficient, but he has an engaging personality and loves to mentor younger developers.

"What about training?" Richard asks,

"I don't think that he would need the full PMI-ACP course, but we can do a two to three day Certified Scrum Master course." Bill replies.

"You think this will be enough?" Richard continues,

"Bhaskal is really sharp, all that he needs is the basics of the Scrum process, and then I can work with him on the rest." Bill says.

"How would the two of you coordinate the project management components?" Richard asks.

"The way that I see it, I will start with all of the documentation, and then handle the traditional Initiation and Planning phases of the project."

"I thought there wasn't a Planning phase with Agile?" Richard inquires.

"Not completely true," Bill replies, "it just is a little bit shorter, and more iterative. But planning still has to take place."

"I see, so continue." Richard says.

"So, once through to the execution phase, that is where I would step back a little and let Bhaskal as Scrum Master manage the day to day operations." Bill says.

"So the daily stand ups and all of that....you would let Bhaskal handle?"

"Exactly." Bill replies. "Then, I would still participate mostly as an observer for the sprint planning and sprint retrospective meetings."

"Makes sense to me." Richard replies.

"It is worth a try. This way we continue business as usual with the project management perspective, we just handle our day to day operations a little bit different.ly."

Richard nods his head as his eyes reflect a piquing of curiosity to see just how well this new idea might work.

CHAPTER 5: Which Project Management Methodology?

"If your actions inspire others to dream more, learn more, do more, and become more, you are a leader"
-John Quincy Adams

Based on the title of this book, and the overall tone, it might be natural for a reader to assume that we would suggest Agile is the best bet for all projects.

Not so fast.

One of the key takeaways that we would love for you as a reader to have after reading our incredible work here is that projects need to be managed the way that **they** need to be managed.

This pseudo-genius observation is meant to stress the fact that no one strategy, no one methodology will work for every type of project or every group of users.

We see this at several clients, the PMO mandates one methodology and it simply does not work all of the time. Instead of viewing a project for having separate and unique needs, a PMO is either a/an "Agile shop" or a "Waterfall shop".

When should we use Waterfall?
Clear Objectives:

In our experience, Waterfall projects are best for endeavors that are static with most of the information known at the very beginning. What we mean by this are projects that are clearly-defined with few variables, such as a hardware configuration project.

Envision a scenario in which a project must be implemented to move a data center from one physical location to another. With this type of a project, there exist so many logistical challenges and disparate groups and individuals that will need to be involved; therefore the project lends itself to a Waterfall approach.

The objectives of this sort of project are fairly evident, and although much discovery would remain to be defined, it is the type of project for which much planning should be invested at the beginning and all of the steps mapped out and put on a Gantt chart.

That example was more of a Hardware-Infrastructure example, so know let's look at a software development example.

Envision a scenario in which there is one subject matter expert-developer on a team and a request comes in for a project with five to six defined enhancements that all fall into the realm of this one subject matter expert's expertise.

It would be impractical to form an agile team around this and therefore dilute this individual's expertise. No, in this case assuming that the enhancements are truly well-defined, this project would be a single-individual Waterfall enhancement project.

Clear Scope and Prioritization:

Another good candidate for a waterfall methodology is a project that has mostly defined scope. This, of course, is difficult to be certain of, but if you as a Project Manager strongly feel that the scope and sequence are fixed and will not be changed, break out the Gantt chart and get to planning.

As all of you current Project Managers probably already know, **very few projects have well-defined scope.**

To continue to hammer home a primary point, this fact is why Agile is such as good idea. So, few projects have obvious, thoroughly defined scope requirements that it makes early planning very difficult.

But, in that ultra-rare occasion in which scope is very thoroughly defined, and the steps well understood, a Waterfall approach can be taken.

Multiple Teams Involved

For projects in which there are a large number of participants, Waterfall methodologies tend to work best. For one reason, as we have already cited, the ideal Agile project team is about 7-9. Beyond that, it becomes nearly impossible to manage in an agile manner.

For teams that cover multiple departments, multiple locations and multiple disciplines, it is far more realistic to use Waterfall for this.

A simple reason for this is that it is basically easier for more people to understand working with a Waterfall Gantt-Chart driven strategy which is what most people are comfortable with.

Also, managing this many people and maintaining this many relationships will be likely more than the Scrum Master and Project Manager can handle, if trying to use Agile.

Now, a potential counter to this would be to break down the overarching project into multiple agile teams and coordinate it this way. Used in such a manner, the Project Manager would almost serve as a Program Manager and link the two agile teams under one umbrella project.

Some of our readers have suggested this approach, and have found it quite successful. To do this, it would require two or more Agile or Scrum teams, two or more Scrum Masters, and one Project Manager that would coordinate all of this into one centralized project plan.

"Brick Wall" Deadlines:

Brick Wall deadlines are dates that your project must make or there will be some severe consequence. These dates can be mandated by upper management or mandated to the company due to reasons such as federal or state compliance.

Upper management may have provided a brick wall deadline, such as the need to complete before the fiscal quarter. In this case, Waterfall is recommended.

The reason for this is that with some type of date that is outside of the project team's control, it takes away their flexibility, and therefore, a primary benefit of Agile.

Limited Team Availability:

One of the key tenets of Agile is that it requires a dedicated team at least for the duration of the two-week sprints. Many times there are situations in which the resources needed for the team are not all available at the same time. For this reason, out of necessity, a waterfall approach should be taken.

Project Type:

We feel that software development works best with Agile/Scrum or AgilePM2020, but other types of projects simply do not. Infrastructure projects, for example, do not really work in an Agile environment. Infrastructure projects include the following:

- Adding physical servers
- Cloud projects
- Database server upgrades

- Data center moves
- Virtualization projects

When should Agile be used?

In general, Agile should be predominantly used for software development projects. Most software development projects by definition have loosely defined objectives which warrant much discussion, review, and iteration before they are right.

Many projects have been well-planned, very thorough and complete, yet failed miserably. The single reason for this was that the features developed for this project were simply not needed. The projects went over budget trying to complete every single function, report, and bell and whistle on the project plan.

Know your Users: Do they change their mind frequently?

One piece of common sense advice is that if a group of users are notorious for changing their requirements frequently, communicating poorly, or otherwise being inconsistent, then it might be wise to opt for an agile approach.

The 80/20 Rule:

The 80/20 rule applies very nicely to software development.

The 80/20 rule loosely defined states that (in our case)

20% of the software features are used 80% of the time

If this is the case, why not do this 20% FIRST and then get to the other features later, if at all?

Obviously, this is an oversimplification but in many cases, at a minimum, 40% of the original project scope should ever be really completed.

This is why we recommend Agile and AgilePM2020 for software development projects.

For an Agile software development project, it would be very easy just to focus on that key 20% of the functionality, roll this into production, and then the business might actually recognize that they don't need the other features.

Statistics state that for most software projects, almost half of all features are either never or rarely ever used. Imagine if a project process could enable these features to not be developed, or at the very least developed later in the project when the business has already received what they were really after.

At this point, the business could decide to drop these features, continue with new features, or let the project conclude early. Either way, the business will more likely than not be happier than if they had waited say 9 months for a very thorough, very complete, yet very unused application was delivered to them.

Team is Available and Defined:

Agile works best when a team is available and well defined. If a solid team is not available for the time required, or if the team does not have the experience required, then Agile will not work.

Comparing Waterfall to Agile:

In the phases of a traditional waterfall development arc, the project moves to the next phase only when the previous phase has been completed.

These six stages apparently resemble a waterfall in some way or another.

With Agile software development, you use an empirical control method, which is a process that is based on the **realities** observed in the actual project.

This involves the following:

- Transparency
- Frequent Inspection
- Adaptation

So, when evaluating the project pipeline, it is very important to plan a management strategy for each project to meet the specific needs of both the project and the user base.

We will discuss specific project examples and then make recommendations on how to manage in a later chapter in this book

For now, let's discuss the strategy and structure for configuring our project team including how to effectively use outsourcing, how to improve communication and then ultimately how to put all of this together for a successful PMO strategy.

David B. Twilley, PMP, CSM

Evaluating the Project Pipeline:

Here is a current example of a project pipeline and the PMO decision what Project management methodology to implement:

Hedge Management System	Agile
DataCenter Move	Waterfall
SAP Upgrade Project	Waterfall
Phased P2V Physical to Virtual Server Changes	Either (because a phased approach is planned)
New Value at Risk Engine	Agile
Adding a new physical plant to network	Waterfall
SAP ABAP Enhancements	Agile

CASE STUDY:

True Spirit Software and Energy Corporation

The waterfall methodology will most likely need to be maintained for several of the in-progress projects.

Even for some of the newer projects, the internal audit department will continue to review that basic project management documents are maintained and updated.

For this reason, Richard has decided to continue to use traditional Project Managers for all project planning, structure and audit documentation requirements.

Not being all that familiar with the personnel needs of Agile projects, he has decided to defer this decision on additional staffing requirements until they have more information about the specific projects.

A new requirement has come in for a server upgrade project for the software division. They want to buy three new physical servers and then at the same time, install the latest version of the database on to these new servers.

Bill comes into Richard's office to discuss the new project.

"What do you think about the new Universe Server Upgrade Project?" Richard asks.

"How do you mean, sir?" Bill asks.

"With the CIO's requirement for Agile, is this project something that you realistically think can be handled with an agile approach?" Richard replies.

Bill pauses to think for a moment.

"From what I understand from speaking with the technical architect, most of the requirements are known and well defined."

"No real development or interface testing here either, right?" Richard asks.

"No, not that I am aware of," Bill replies.

"How would you envision managing this project, Bill?" Richard asks.

"I would make the technical architect the project SME, and then let him define the project team which would be a combination of database and server folks."

"How would you coordinate the timeline, the schedule?" Richard asks.

"I would need input from the technical architect, of course, but I would envision this being a sequential, phased approach with well-defined steps." Bill replies.

Richard paces and then shakes his head.

"Sounds like a Waterfall project to me," Richard says.

"Me too," Bill replies. "But I will let **you** tell the CIO." Bill finishes with a smile.

Richard just shakes his head again, fully aware that an awkward conversation is in his near-term future.

CHAPTER 6: Outsourcing 2020

"Businesses are no longer receiving the cost savings from outsourcing that they once did"
-Gerald Chertavian

Allow us to deviate from our initial discussions of project management methodologies, and touch on the issues of outsourcing. The reason that we choose to start this conversation here is that the approach that each company takes towards outsourcing will or should influence their decisions on project management methodologies.

A theme that we will repeat quite frequently here is that we believe that a highly outsourced and offshore model is more conducive to a Waterfall structure than Agile. We see with companies that plan to continue to use off-shore outsourcing as a significant portion of their development, and they try to implement Agile and fail miserably.

This has nothing to do with the outsourced talent, but the very nature of their being in different offices and in different time zones. This lack of a truly collaborative effort renders an Agile strategy less effective.

So, companies need to be honest in their evaluations and strategies. If outsourcing will continue to be a major component of IT projects, simply do not insist on a full Agile adoption. We recommend using Agile with on-site teams and Waterfall with the outsourced teams.

In our view, Outsourcing in the year 2020 will be an even more diverse and truly global affair than it is today. We were surprised to learn exactly how many countries are leaders in the world of IT Outsourcing. Many countries such as The Philippines, Chile, Costa Rica and Brazil offer interesting alternatives to the known IT Outsourcing hubs of India and China.

Certain Eastern European Countries have also become very involved in IT Outsourcing and we feel will continue to be. Companies such as EPAM Systems, with large operations in Ukraine, are examples of the possibilities within this region.

The only barriers that preclude these areas from becoming stronger IT Outsourcing players is the English language. As these countries move forward, however, we feel that the gap will tighten and the English issue will become less of a factor.

In addition, we recommend to several of our clients that they have an internal staff that has multi- language capabilities. We do not feel that difficulty with English should be an issue when working with these outsourcing providers.

For this reason, at True Spirit Consulting, we have on our staff individuals fluent in Spanish, Hindi, Cantonese, and Russian. This way all of the potential partnerships in outsourcing are available to us.

The current leaders in Outsourcing are primarily from countries that you might expect: India and others in Asia. We were a little surprised to see as many cities from the Philippines on the list, and also that Poland made the list.

This only serves to further our point that outsourcing is now, and will only continue to be a global phenomenon, not limited to one or two main countries.

Here is the current list of the top outsourcing cities as of today

Top Outsourcing Cities – 2015

(December 2014)

1. Bangalore, India
2. Manila, Philippines
3. Mumbai, India
4. Delhi, India
5. Chennai, India
6. Hyderabad, India
7. Pune, India
8. Cebu City, Philippines
9. Krakow, Poland
10. Shanghai, China

Based on our research and trending data, this is our subjective estimate on the changes in the Outsourcing provider cities in the next five years. All of this is based on trending, analysis and our evaluation of the results.

1. Bangalore, India
2. Manila, The Philippines
3. Mumbai, India
4. Delhi, India
5. Santiago, Chile
6. San Jose, Costa Rica
7. Dublin, Ireland
8. Pune, India
9. Shanghai, China
10. Prague, Czech Republic

What might catch your eye about this list is that even though India still has almost half of the top10 spots, this is down from the current numbers in which it dominates, owning 6-7 of the top 10, depending on which survey cited.

In our opinion, India will continue to lead in the IT outsourcing arena, but their edge will start to slowly fade. India dominates now because their consultancies are more entrenched and have better lobbying efforts in Washington.

We find the so-called "Near Shoring" countries of Latin America to be great potential areas for growth. Countries such as Chile and Costa Rica, which are stable, have educated workforces, and are likely more ambitious about taking on outsourcing responsibilities and would welcome the opportunity.

One of the major reasons that we like the near shoring countries is also linked to geographic proximity, which puts these areas in similar time zones as most U.S offices. To us, this is a top priority if we are going to use outsourcing. We cannot endorse this sort of "black-box" outsourcing where we never hear from our outsourcing workers except through their "handler" or on-site consultancy manager, who has his company's interests at heart, not yours.

Time Zone Factors:

In our experience, time zones can be a critical component of evaluating a potential outsourcing partner.

For this reason, companies that we have worked with looked more towards companies who operate in countries closer in time zone compatibility with the United States.

This puts countries such as Chile and Costa Rica in consideration and gives them an advantage as their time zones are significantly closer to that of the US than similar outsourcing locations such as Europe and India.

Chile, for example, is two hours ahead of the Eastern time zone and only five ahead of the Pacific time zone. This differs with India, which is a full 10.5 hours ahead of Eastern and over 13.5 hours ahead of the Pacific time zone.

Collaboration in real time is therefore rendered impossible by this disconnect of working times.

For Agile, we want teams that can work on a daily basis and therefore should look for offshore resources that more clearly align with the core business hours for our development team.

Optimizing Time Zone Differences:

One of the more innovative solutions to this time zone issue was one in which teams were coordinated to create almost an all-day development cycle.

The primary development and agile team was located in California. This team would coordinate with the Chile offshore folks for development and then the Bangalore-based Indian team would take the daily development work and apply the QA testing steps and then return to the Chile team for more work.

The cycle worked like this:

1. Chile team initiates development
2. California (Primary) team works on the daily coding efforts
3. California team passes to Bangalore team for QA
4. At end of their day, Bangalore team passes back to Chile team for next development cycle

But Why Does This Matter?

Time and time again, we have heard the argument that it should not matter which time zone that a development or support team resides provided the work continues to get done.

Well, we agree and disagree.

For support staff, such as help desk and customer service, we could not agree more, it does not matter where the teams are physically located to get their work done.

This is true because their work is essentially individual driven and independent. For the most part, they do not function, nor need they function as a part of a larger team.

Development teams, on the other hand, really need to be able to work collectively and pool knowledge and resources. As we have stressed over and over in this book, Project Management 2020 is all about collective execution, teamwork, and collaboration.

Our recommendation is for collocation whenever possible, but when this is not feasible; if nothing else teams should operate in the same time zone, or with the same work hours.

But we cannot do that, we have a disparate team located across the Globe in multiple time zones:

OK, then the need exists to become a little bit more creative. I don't feel that this is a deal-breaker, it simply involves a little bit more innovation and outside of the box thinking.

What we have done in the past when dealing with outside time zone staff is to have two team members on the project work in parallel with this staff, if nothing more than to coincide on one or two work hours. This enables the daily status to be reported to team members who will then relay all of this information to the larger project team.

Some teams manage this by using a single individual to coordinate this, but we have found this to be a mistake, as this single individual can sometimes themselves become a bottleneck of information and also (and especially if they are from the same company as the off-shore staff) they can cover for the offshore team members and mask any deficiencies.

We don't want any of that. The entire premise of this type of Project Management is full transparency. There is no way we are going to hide poor performing team members and then attempt to make up for it later. This is called "technical debt" and we simply cannot allow it to happen with active project management.

Outsourcing and Agile:

Our opinion is that it is very difficult to outsource Agile. I have read several white papers that site example after example in which it has been a success, but that is still not convincing me. It takes more than a few successful projects to deviate from a core tenet of Agile, which is development with a team, in a collocated team environment.

Agile works best with a strong team that works together, at one place, in a similar time zone, and with the same clear objectives. Outsourcing just does not work for Agile.

For companies that have incorporated offshore outsourcing as a large percentage of their staff, then re-think using Agile as your primary Project Management methodology.

Are we still getting the "Top Talent"?

We have spoken to several companies who have expressed concerns that the Indian outsourcing market has become too expensive and saturated. They note that the quality of talent is not what was about 4-5 years ago. Furthermore, these consulting firms with strong reputations and influence often have far more work than they have qualified personnel to perform it.

As a result of this, these clients have reported to us that these workers were not as qualified as they claimed to be on their resumes/CVs and the projects suffer as a result. It is very difficult to properly vet and offshore resource without the opportunity to interview them.

What is puzzling is that these resources are accepted with no real interview, no significant vetting process, basically only the word of the consulting manager to support these people and their claimed skills.

Vetting Offshore Resources:

For companies we consult with, we have advised an extra step in the vetting process for the offshore technical resources. This is true regardless of the location of the outsourcing but is very important to ensure that you are getting what you are paying for.

As part of this vetting, we have a conference call and preferably a WebEx or comparable type meeting in which we look for two main things:

1. Does this individual have the requisite communication skills to work with our team?
2. Does this individual have the requisite technical and business skills to work with our team?

Now if the consulting manager insists on being in this meeting, that is a red flag right there. If the consulting manager also then proceeds to do most of the talking, then that is the second red flag and in our opinions an automatic "No".

What this tells us is that this interviewee is likely a very junior person that this consultancy will bill as a senior, and they hope to have several senior individuals mentor this junior resource to enable them to bill at a higher rate.

We have heard hundreds of horror stories of similar instances, and really don't feel too much sympathy for the companies, because they let it happen.

We think that there is definitely a place for outsourcing, but just as we cannot recommend Agile as the one and only project management methodology, we also cannot endorse outsourcing as the solution to IT budget issues.

In our opinion, outsourcing works as a supplement to your existing, core IT project teams. Use outsourced resources for those tasks that are well defined, finite, and time-boxed.

If you are an IT Manager, you should advise that certain fixed milestones and deliverables are required at certain time intervals, and have either daily or weekly status and progress reports to help alleviate any potential abuses.

Optimizing Outsourcing in your Enterprise:

Outsourcing is a reality of life and we are not intending to sound like we are against it, moreover we are more of a proponent of strategic use of outsourcing and not a complete adoption of outsourcing to replace your on site staff.

We recommend that outsourcing be used to strategically augment your current staff and used in a manner that supports your projects and your business teams.

One fact that we have learned over the years is that certain groups of business users do not have the patience to work with individuals who do not communicate well, nor do they understand certain details of the business.

Outsourcing resources are great for completing tasks, development, quality assurance, but cannot be realistically expected to understand the business, the politics and the nuances of your specific enterprise.

Outsourcing with Agile Software Development:

We are fairly consistent with this theme, but we will repeat for the purposes of clarification: *Agile and outsourcing don't work well together.*

When we say this, we are referring to using outsourced offshore team members as a part of the core agile development team.

The reasons that we say that this is a bad idea really comes down to the entire collaborative nature of Agile development. Without the ability to work on the same time schedules and collaborate on a day to day basis, it is very difficult to work in an Agile capacity.

One idea that we have seen work very successfully is utilizing offshore resources in a QA capacity for supplemental support to the primary IT Agile project team.

It would work something like this:

1. Agile team does development work
2. Passes code for review to offshore team
3. In the morning, offshore team has returned testing results
4. Development team continues the cycle

Outsourcing with Waterfall:

As much as we don't care for using outsourcing teams with an Agile approach, we feel that they are perfectly suited for Waterfall projects.

This is part of why we feel that the Agile Project Management 2020 strategy is the realistic strategy for most companies.

Most companies that push Agile as their sole project management methodology also have a heavy offshore outsourcing component.

Therefore, they are trying to accomplish something that we are noting here, goes against the basic tenets of Agile and Scrum, which is to have defined, collocated teams.

For Waterfall projects, however, we think outsourcing can be used for half of the project team at least. These tasks can be time-boxed and coordinated in such a manner that the specific time zone availability of the team really does not matter.

For this reason, upon the initial project pipeline review, we recommend that these outsourced off shore resources be tasked with projects such as this.

Outsourcing Conclusion:

Outsourcing is here to stay for a majority of companies.

The perceived savings and optimization is too strong to go away any time soon.

Having said that, we advise that companies take a holistic and strategic approach to their outsourcing and use resources as appropriate for each individual project.

IT Directors and PMO Managers should have the discretion to use project resources as they deem them appropriate for each specific project and not because of some imperial corporate mandate.

Our recommendations are as follows for outsourcing:

1. Use onsite or near-shoring teams for Agile projects
2. If they must be used for Agile, use offshore resources for QA and other non-team or time sensitive tasks to maximize the development cycle
3. Use offshore resources primarily for Waterfall projects, for which their time can be optimized and their tasks can be completed outside of the two week time boxed sprints that are requirements in Agile.
4. Experiment with an around-the-clock dynamic by locating off shore resources in a different region. If you coordinate it properly, supplementing with offshore teams could provide an almost 24 hour development cycle.

David B. Twilley, PMP, CSM

CASE STUDY:

True Spirit Software and Energy Corporation

As a software development company, True Spirit has multiple outsourcing vendors providing a significant amount of offshore development work.

Its primary software development team is located in the US at the West Coast corporate headquarters, but the secondary software development team is located in India, along with a QA/Testing team located in the Philippines.

Both of these outsourcing vendors have multiple year contracts and cannot simply be phased out immediately.

Patty, the CIO has a conversation with Richard about outsourcing and its role in the new agile conversion.

"How well can we work with the existing outsourcing teams in so far as an agile strategy is concerned?" Patty asks.

Richard pauses before responding.

"I think I have some concerns there." He replies.

"How so?" Patty asks.

"I think for our fully offshore teams, they are so used to running on their own, that any attempt to bring them under the agile team strategy would be difficult."

"But can it be done?" Patty asks.

"I think it can, but only in a short term manner." Richard replies.

"How about this," Patty proposes. "Let's use the outsourcing teams as secondary agile teams and have them coordinate with the onsite teams."

"So have them work on separate projects?" Richard asks.

"Yes, I do realize that the entire team nature of Agile requires for the team to be able to collaborate, and this does not work with outsourced teams." Patty replies.

"I agree. I would also like to propose one other change." Richard adds.

"What is that?" Patty inquires.

"Let's add a new outsourced team that we can use to work with our local teams, and have them in or close to the same working time zone."

"Somewhere in Latin America?" Patty asks.

"Exactly. I have worked with a consultancy in Chile and one in Costa Rica that would provide us a set of outsourced resources that can work more closely to our times." Richard says.

"Ok. Check in to that and give me some numbers by the end of the week." Patty replies.

Richard is pleased, since he already has a statement of work ready to go for six offshore resources from Chile.

"What about the **existing** outsourcing team that we have in India, we still need to keep them involved and busy, right?" Patty asks.

"Absolutely," Richard replies, "but we have to figure out what types of projects that we can use them for."

"What about projects such as Infrastructure and more static items?" Patty asks.

Richard hesitates and then responds.

"I was thinking more like using them as a supplement to the Agile team, to do some testing and things of that nature."

"Testing?" Patty asks.

"Yes," Richard replies, "I was speaking with Bhaskal and some of the technical guys and they envision a scenario in which the team could develop the code during the day here locally, and then at the end of the day pass it on to the offshore team for QA and testing and then have it back for the development team in the morning."

Patty pauses, scratches her forehead like she is thinking.

"If we did that, it seems like we would have almost a full day operation." Patty says,

"Exactly," Richard replies, "and this way the time zone issues are not a problem, and actually work to our benefit."

"That is an intriguing idea, I must admit." Patty concedes.

"It gets better," Richard adds, "by adding the resources from Latin America, it allows us to get even closer to a 24-hour operation."

"How so?" Patty asks.

Richard takes out his tablet PC and shows it to Patty. On it, he has the web site www.timeanddate.com loaded and displayed.

"Here, if you look at this," Richard says, "with our offices in the US Pacific time zone, and the offices in Santiago, Chile, they are five hours ahead of us."

"So? How does that help us?" Patty adds, challengingly.

"I was thinking that in an ideal situation, we could have a three pronged approach. The US team would develop, and at end of day pass this to the Indian QA team, and then they can pass it to the Chile development team to start a full five hours before our team ever gets to the office."

Patty does not reply initially, but then looks interested in this suggestion.

"It seems that we would be far more productive this way." Patty says.

"Absolutely, we would," Richard replies. "And then, once the Chile team leaves for the day, they can have a meeting and do a hand-off with the California team."

Patty nods and starts to walk off, "I like that idea."

"One final question and I will let you get back to it." Patty says, "What about those hard core development types that would not be content with just doing QA work?"

"Right," Richard responds, "for those people, I wanted to continue to work with them on non Agile projects."

"Oh, that makes sense I suppose." Patty replies, "I will leave that to your discretion, but one way or another, we have to keep those guys engaged."

"Thanks, Patty, we will make it happen." Richard says.

CHAPTER 7: Communication Plan 2020

"The single biggest problem in communication is the illusion that it has taken place."
--George Bernard Shaw

Just one person's opinion, but in all of the discussion of methodologies, teams, and analytics it comes down to this statement:

Communication is the one skill without which a project manager cannot succeed.

How many times have we as Project Managers been in this position? What was clearly understood by some is not understood by the person that matters most, and big issues result from this.

In our opinion, the most important responsibility of a Project Manager is communication.

In a recent survey of our clients, a clear pattern began to emerge citing the difference in successful and unsuccessful projects.

For the successful projects, the Project Managers all created an environment that fostered good two-way communication. I want to stress one key point here: the most important thing is not to just provide updates and talk, but make sure that you as a Project Manager are available to listen.

Several of my Project Manager colleagues are excellent talkers. They command a room and have that type of voice that a radio DJ would envy. They sound like a defense attorney that only a millionaire could afford to have on retainer.

But they can't *listen* to save their lives. They are so "on" all of the time, working the charm, etc, that listening to the input of others becomes difficult for them.

Be sure to provide information but also to do a good job of *eliciting* good information. In other words, be not just a good, but a great listener. This simple fact can make or break your project.

So, in our survey of over 50 clients the emerging four traits for successful projects involved the Project Managers:

- Maintain a clear communication schedule
- Communicate clearly to where it is understood
- Talk to stakeholders early and keep them engaged
- Create a communication channel by which stakeholders can reach the PM individually rather than have to speak in front of others in a meeting

On the flip side of these positive traits, the negative patterns that emerged included the following:

Failing projects had these traits:

- Full evaluation of the project communication needs
- Understanding how the information was received
- Two-way communication (poor listening)

As a Project Manager, I definitely have made these mistakes in the past and learned from them. What is very difficult for any individual is to understand how communication is received.

How are we supposed to be inside someone else's head to understand what they heard? This is impossible, which makes the repetitive nature of project communication so necessary. I have a personality trait that I am sure annoys many people, in that I repeat myself many times.

Not like a parrot or anything where I say it twice in a row, but I will say something once, and then close out the point by summarizing the key point. Sometimes people will poke fun at this habit (rightly so), but one thing that does happen is that *the point gets made.*

Another positive habit I have learned helps to address the issue of understanding how information was received was to follow up any status updates with a simple Q&A session(for meetings) and then follow up with people individually to ask them if they have any questions about the update that I provided.

Many times people are too shy or are embarrassed to ask clarifying questions, or as I call them, "questions of confirmation" in which the person believes that they know the answer but they still want some reassurance. As the Project Manager, be there to reassure them, that is a great part of the responsibility of the project manager.

Many of my friends have been stunned that their projects that were running really well, under budget and ahead of schedule were perceived as failures by the business. The reason for this turned out to be one or two displeased stakeholders that had been confused by the project progress, made some false assumptions and then spread negative gossip about the project all over.

Communication is the one skill without which a project manager cannot succeed. (see I repeated that too)

Now this is not exactly a new revelation, yet still you would be surprised how often communication is overlooked as a key project management component.

Here are our guidelines for managing Project Management communication

Three Rules For Project Management Communication

1. Full transparency – keep no secrets
2. Identify and select the proper communication method
3. Centralized project status

Types of Communication:

The primary types of communication are as follows:

- Documentation
- In-person
- Phone
- Email
- Instant Message/Chat

Taking it a step further we would like to differentiate between active and passive communication types and point out when it may be appropriate to use one over the other.

Passive communication might be fine in the middle of the project for redundant updates such as weekly status reports. For working with a project team, and especially building and developing a relationship with the project team, it is important to use more active communication methods.

One of the absolute most important things that can be done is to identify the correct communication method for the specific projects, specific stakeholders and the current state of the project.

In this table, we identify the primary communication methods, evaluate if the method is passive or active, and rank it in order of our preference.

Communication Methods and Recommendations:

Communication	Passive/Active	Preference
In-Person	Active	1
Phone	Active	2
I.M/Chat	Active	3
E-Mail	Passive	4
Documentation	Passive	5

To us, there is nothing better for fostering a good project relationship than good in-person communication. This could be nothing more than a 5-minute chat or maybe it extends into an hour impromptu discussion with the project sponsor. The benefits of in-person communications are somewhat obvious, but for a project manager especially it clearly conveys your involvement and level of commitment to the others on the team.

Another good form of active communication is a simple phone call. When a quick update should be provided or a question asked, I don't recommend leaving this to an email. An Email to me is something that may or may not be read and responded to. We all receive so many unwanted emails that why add another to the inbox.

If a significant update is to be provided, or a question asked especially of the project sponsor or product owner, try the in-person first and if that can't happen try the phone call or instant message.

Instant Messaging/Chat is a good mechanism also, but again should only be used after the phone call is attempted, because like emails, people tend to work with numerous chat windows open simultaneously, and may not see the message or feel like responding to it.

And finally the passive communication types of Email and documentation. Emails, as noted earlier, are primarily good for generic updates and to confirm items discussed through other means. One **great** use of email is that of a paper trail.

As I started in my Project Management career, I far preferred the in-person communication mechanism. I would speak with my team, talk to the business and in my mind everything was fine and understandings were in place.

I would **not** follow up with an email to summarize what we had discussed, and in absence of proof to the contrary, those verbal agreements could be denied.

One of my colleagues showed me how he would always immediately return from any kind of meeting or in-person discussion and send a follow up email to summarize what was agreed upon, thereby creating a paper trail if needed later.

The email would be a simple format such as this:

Mr. Ballenger,

Thanks for spending the time to discuss the project plan today. To summarize what we discussed, you are okay with the following changes:

--Move UAT back two weeks

--Add Lisa to the testing team

--Request to please provide Donuts for the project team every Friday from now on

Thanks,

Dave

Just as an aside, that donut thing actually worked.

Communication Frequency:

This is the area in which a Project Manager needs to do a better job of reading people. As the project proceeds, we need to be able to identify and anticipate what the communication needs are that goes *beyond* the Communication Plan.

The Communication Plan is simply a guideline, because at the beginning of the project things are fine, and nobody expects that they will need daily updates or hand-holding, but by the end of the project often times that is what you get.

As we work with a Project Sponsor, we do a couple of things:

- We observe how engaged they are with the project
- We ask other Project Managers how they have worked with them in the past
- We watch them for participation in status meetings.
- We notice if they respond to the status emails.

So, will all of this, what should happen next?

What you want to do is to increase the amount of communication to the point at which the project sponsor is satisfied. One piece of advice that we share is that communication should increase incrementally as the project moves forward.

What we are saying is that the more progress that you make, the more this needs to be communicated accordingly.

One of the worst things that can happen to a project is ironically when the project is proceeding well, but an anxious project sponsor is under the false impression that it is NOT. Unfortunately, once this impression is created, it takes triple the effort to correct this false impression, *if that impression can be changed at all!*

To prevent this, we make sure to broadcast key accomplishments early and often. We visit project sponsors at their desk just to give them informal updates, and also allow for them to ask any questions. Sometimes we even get to the point that they ask us not to bother them.

You know what, that is OK. Problems do not occur when the Project Manager is **too engaged,** no problems occur when the Project Manager makes assumptions that the business and the team are on the same page.

Here is our recommendation with increasing communication and identifying ideal times for it to occur.

Project Role	Status Meeting	In-Person Visit
Project Sponsor	Monday	Friday
Key Stakeholder	Monday	Wednesday
Key Stakeholder	Monday	Thursday

Our objective here is to manage the impression of the project. The impression of the project in the minds of these three business users is that we are involved, caring, and making great progress.

As noted in the quote to start the chapter, "the single biggest problem about communication, is the illusion that it is taking place". We cannot assume that each of these individuals speak to one another or read all of the status emails. We must take control of the communication and **own** the process.

Types of Communication – Summarized:

So by now we know all of the communication methods, have discussed differences between active and passive communication types, and have discussed the frequency of communication also.

One other recommendation that we have, which we have used to great success is posting a centralized project summary in a network location:

This document is to be updated daily with as much detail as deemed necessary with the objective being that it serves as an executive summary of sorts.

Where this really helps is when a business project team member moves off the project and is replaced. Now, with this document they can immediately see exactly what is going on and get a snapshot view of the project progress.

This differs with status reports, especially since this new project team member would not have access to all of the cumulative status reports over the duration of the project.

I will not give you a sample document here because that is for each client to define

For Status reports, make sure that this is communicated to cover the key points

- The Work Tasks – How it is to be done
- The Objectives – why it is being done
- Timeline – when it is being done
- Cost – how much did we budget, where are we as a percentage
- Stakeholders – who is involved and what are they doing

We are big fans of simplicity and feel that for certain audiences, the most basic type of status report works the best.

If you are familiar with the concept of the One-Page Project Manager, then following a similar type of approach might work well, especially when dealing with upper-level C-Level managers.

As we said before, and will repeat over and over: Communication is the one skill without which a project manager cannot succeed.

Communicating Major Changes:

In our case study in an earlier chapter, we encountered a scenario in which business stakeholder Jim Ballenger became very irate partially because he was given misinformation.

This lack of information can be almost as damaging as someone actually receiving erroneous information.

A colleague once told me that "in absence of proof to the contrary, many times people will assume the worst to be true."

So, a good rule of thumb for implementing major changes that will affect multiple groups of stakeholders is to provide the information to them early, create an open discussion forum and do not blind-side people with sudden changes that they were not informed about.

Ideally, as in our case study, the CIO would have had the communication with her C-level colleagues and they would have relayed it to their direct reports.

In our case, this did not happen and as a result the big issue occurred with displeased stakeholder, Jim Ballenger and now more damage control needs to be done, as in our current installment of our case study on the next page.

CASE STUDY:

True Spirit Software and Energy Corporation Communication Plan 2020:

For Richard, the PMO Manager, the biggest challenge in regards to communication is the overall communication to the business and the team regarding the new project management methodology.

He works with Bill and Craig to define a strategy to notify the business about the methodology change and they all three work together to craft a plan to increase the frequency and complexity of communication for the next year during this change period.

While Bill and Craig work to define the specifics, Richard takes a proactive approach and meets with the most influential and most outspoken critic about the new plan, the VP of Energy Trading, Jim Ballenger.

Listen in, as Richard explains the new process to a fairly reluctant business user.

"Thanks for joining me here Jim." Richard says, as Jim Ballenger walks into his office.

"Cut the pleasantry bullshit, Richard, what is all of this shit I am hearing about my projects taking longer to complete?" Jim says.

"What do you mean *taking longer?*" Richard asks.

"With the CIO's requirement for Agile, is this project something that you realistically think can be handled with an

"This Agile bullshit, as I understand it, we will need to wait until everybody learns this new fancy project management thing before we start any new projects."

"Who told you that?" Richard asks.

"One of your own guys, Steve, he says that this new methodology will take longer and make all of our lives more difficult." Jim finishes.

Richard is stunned, here one of his own team members has gone against him and is working to sabotage the efforts with the business. Richard realizes that if Ballenger is opposed to it, that he can completely shut down this entire effort, considering how connected and influential he is with other business users.

Then the CIO would hold Richard personally responsible for the failure.

After a momentary pause, Richard regains his composure and continues.

"I understand Steve's position," Richard replies like a cool politician under fire, "he has expressed these concerns to me as well. I must admit that I am a little disappointed that he has chosen to come to you about this rather than going through proper channels."

"So you are admitting that he is right?" Ballenger continues,

"No, not at all. Let me explain how this will work." Richard replies.

"You have my attention." Ballenger replies.

Richard proceeds to spend the next thirty minutes telling Ballenger about how projects will actually be developed more quickly with agile, and how the teams will be developed to suit the specific projects individually based on their needs, and assign individuals based upon their qualifications.

After the conversation, Ballenger's anger and resistance seem to have at least partially abated, and he admits as much to Richard.

"Thank you for the explanation," Jim says. "I am still not completely sold on the idea, I generally don't want any negative changes, but I will give you guys the benefit of the doubt and see what you come up with."

"Thanks, Jim, I appreciate it," Richard says.

As Jim stands up and leaves his office, Richard realizes that he has two problems:

His team must quickly act to persuade the business(and especially Jim Ballenger) that the new strategy will benefit them

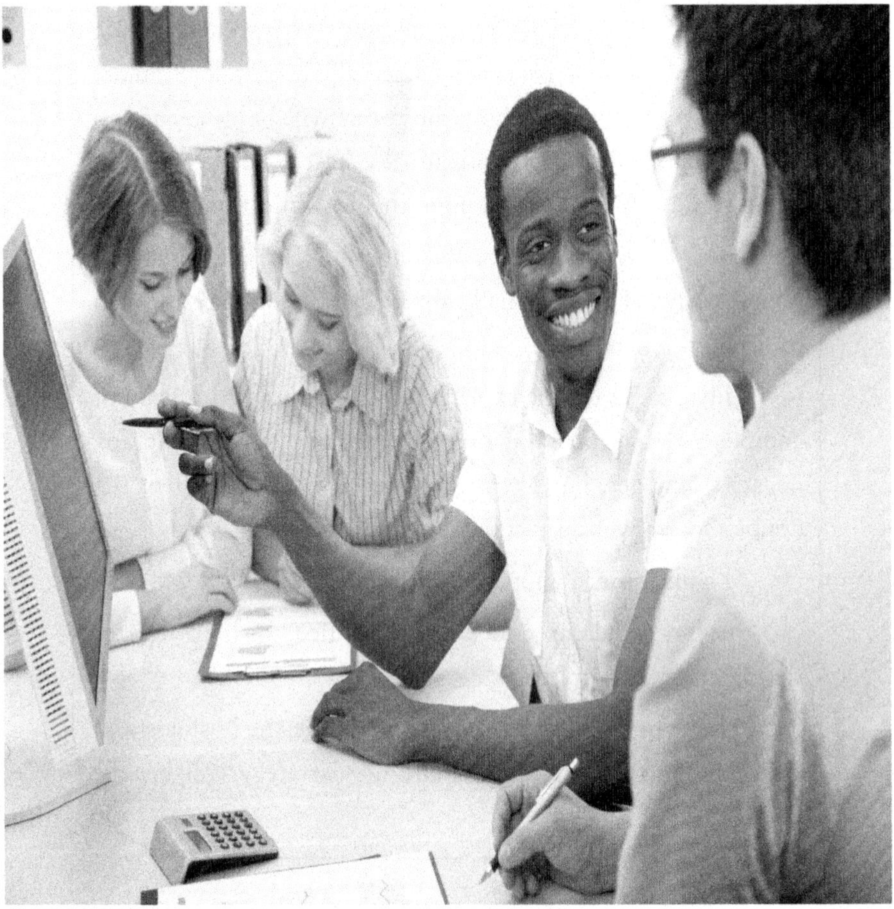

CHAPTER 8: Building The Perfect Team

"People tend to work in teams, in a collaborative way, in an informal network. If you create an environment like that, it's much more effective and much more efficient."
--Jim Mitchell

Now we want to discuss the idea of building a solid team. In this usage, we are referring to the overall PMO/IT Department staff and then we will also discuss how to manage teams during Agile iterations, etc.

The Ideal Team:
Elements of a Great Team:

What are we looking for when we talk about building a great team?

We want individuals with drive, creativity, and technical skills that can work well with others and be solid contributors.

An ideal team has the following characteristics:

- Diverse Group of individual talents
- Share common goal and vision
- Like learning new things

- Enjoy working together
- Loyal to the project

Of course, as we all know there is no truly realistic ideal team. What we have to do is to do the most with what we have. That may be true, but as we develop and expand, we should always be looking to develop and recruit a team with the characteristics that work best for us.

Characteristics that we recommend in all team members are as follows:

Role	Traits	Skills
Project Manager	Good communicator, consensus builder, organized	Technical and Analytical skills. Communication. PMP and CSM Certifications
Scrum Master	Leader and Hard Worker	Technical and Communication. CSM or will provide for them
On Site Developers	Team Oriented, Good Communicator	Technical Skills, Cross-Functional skills
Offshore Developers	Team Oriented, Good Communicator, works on fixed duration items, preferably short term	Technical Skills
Product Owner	Leader, Organized, Influencial with the Business	Solid business knowledge with some technical understanding

Organizations Need to Develop Teams:

All companies or organizations have their own limitations on what they can do with staffing. Some are committed to the outsourcing model, some have a mixture of outsourcing and internal resources, and some are all internal resources.

Within these limitations, organizations must then work to maximize the development of these team members and not simply view them as **resources**. In our ideal AgilePM2020 vision, we develop team members that improve each project and are continually adding to their skill sets. The only way that this can happen is if management enables and supports it, which is one of our key recommendations in AgilePM2020.

As we have already discussed, Project Managers should learn the technology, strong technical leads should have the opportunity to work in a Scrum Master role. But don't stop there, several technical people are always looking to learn new skills and take on new responsibilities. Be empowering of this and support it.

A Culture of Mentoring Not Finger-Pointing:

Another point that should be made here is that our intention when running projects with this strong team approach is that we want to build a strong team and that does not always mean **starting** off with a good team.

What we mean by that is that you should ideally aim for a good mixture of more senior staff along with some junior team members who are energetic and willing to learn. We should not be looking to point out any technical weaknesses or personal failing here. Instead, we need to apply a mentoring and coaching approach by which we help our team members develop and build their skills and improve accordingly.

I have worked on several projects in which a developer had, for example, strength in Java development but they are assigned to work a project in SAP ABAP. The project starts and this developer is out of his element and underperforming due to his lack of familiarity with SAP. Nobody volunteers to help him and he feels completely lost.

Rather than ask what can be done to help, the Project Manager goes to this developer's manager and they complain about his performance.

Now, what good does this do? This culture of passing blame, critiquing, finger-pointing and tattle-telling might help a project manager deflect blame in the *short term* but in the long term it is self-destructive.

Word of this will surely spread, and now this developer and his many colleagues are aware of how this Project Manager operates. Who then would want to work on a project with this person?

In our opinion, very few if any people would want to work for this Project Manager.

Developing the Sprint Team:

Without question, one of the most difficult balancing acts is being the strict project manager who has to manage deadlines and command respect and then also being the team leader who is still a **part** of the team and wants them to succeed as a group.

What we propose in team building is, as noted before, have a wide array of skill levels and career levels on your teams. Assign tasks to the entire team, and at a minimum have two people collaborate on a single task at any one time.

If they want to split it up at a certain level that is fine, but by pairing these people together, you accomplish a few things. First, you encourage collaboration, and secondly you likely improve the speed of completion as the two will feel pushed by the other and will not want to lag behind.

We Have a Team Member Who Just Is Not Contributing, What Can We Do Then?

Yes, there is a certain point at which nothing more can be done to deal with a team member who is not contributing. There are two main categories of problem team members in our view, the *contrarian/nonteam player* and the *technically-challenged*.

For us, we have more of an issue with the contrarian/non team player than one who is technically challenged. For the contrarian, this is the type of person who may not contribute in the stand-up meetings. Maybe they speak negatively about the project or show no interest in working in a team environment.

In my projects, I have known and worked with multiple individuals who are geniuses and absolutely brilliant, not just a dumb PM such as myself. I would not, however, want these individuals on my project team because I know that they would not ever care to work in this **team** environment.

These technical experts feel secure in their position due either to tenure or perceived proprietary knowledge that they possess. For an individual such as this that is on the project team and being very disruptive, this is the scenario in which we recommend approaching the person's manager and suggesting that this person be removed from the project team.

For the underperformer, again first we strongly recommend a team mentoring approach before anything else. If mentoring has been provided, assistance and training where necessary, and the person still does not perform, at that point approach the manager to have this person removed.

Sprint Rotations:

One mechanism that we have used in the past to great success to avoid offending those team members that we would rather not use anymore is the rotating sprint team.

We will discuss in greater detail later, but the rotating Sprint team enables the project manager to accommodate personal time off, vacations, scheduling conflicts, etc by scheduling a certain team to each sprint from a larger overall pool.

For our purposes here, we can simply phase out the underperformers by not having them be in any additional sprints.

This does key on the assumption that as a project manager this flexibility in staff is available, but in most mid to large sized shops a project manager should have this flexibility.

Building a strong team is a continuous effort. It is not always easy, and not always immediately successful. There will be under performers, individuals that can improve and also some people who are just not team players.

The goal of the Project Manager should be to build teams and give them as many opportunities to succeed as possible. The first response should never be one of hostility or criticism, Project Managers need to remember that they do not *command* the team, just organize and lead.

Team Development and Skill Enhancements:

Not to quote specific statistics, but it is well known in marketing that it is far more expensive to get a new customer than to retain an existing customer. Some estimates put the multiplier as high as 30 times more expensive.

Now, while it is not an exact comparison, an argument can be made that it is equally important to maintain and develop a solid team that works well together, develops and is committed for the long term.

We realize that the days of corporations and workers having a 25-30 year relationship that leads straight to retirement are over, but still there are many ways to develop a core team and retain them.

Once a department has recognized its team, the way we envision it, there are two types of team members: core team members and skills-based resources.

Skills-based resources would apply to individuals who are there because of their skills only, and for whom there is no envisioned promotion or upward mobility. This would be contractors, outsourced resources, interns, etc.

Core team members are those that should be groomed, developed and maintained. And while a full discussion of this topic is beyond the reach of this book, it bears mentioning.

Especially when implementing a change such as switching from Waterfall to Agile, time and expense should be allocated for the appropriate development, training and other opportunities to enable individuals to cross train.

For Agile purposes, and general project management perspective, provide options to core team members such as:

- PMI – ACP training
- PMP Boot camp training courses
- Certified Scrum Master Courses
- Lean Six Sigma Yellow, Green, and Black Belt programs

We are realistic, and do realize there are people out there who will take advantage of these opportunities to leave for greener pastures. But for each of those who do this, we feel that there are several others who would appreciate the company's investment in their development and their future and repay them accordingly with corresponding loyalty.

Team Building Ideas:

We have seen several good team building exercises used at various companies in the past to varying degrees of success.

The key point is for the Project Manager to do whatever they can do to motivate the team, which typically involves being a part of it and not trying to rule over it.

In addition to simple good will, another objective is to build an environment that takes care of most human needs and minimizes the need for the team to leave during the day.

Sometimes this is limited by the overall corporate environment, but in my consulting experience the most productivity has been in environments in which team members don't have to go off site for breakfast, lunch, or if you are working late, dinners.

Basic needs such as beverages, snacks, meal items should be easy to get and made available to team members.

The amount spent on such items can be quickly recouped with increases in productivity.

In our consulting experience, we have learned that about two-thirds of the time, people would rather NOT have to leave to get lunch, snacks, coffee etc, but are simply forced to due to lack of options in their work location.

As a Project Manager, you cannot always control this, but within budgetary limitations, there are things that can be done to improve morale and create a more productive work environment for your teams.

Simple things that a Project manager can do to help the team or keep the atmosphere productive include:

- **Afternoon Gourmet Coffee Hour** – I worked at a company once, and a group of us would rotate brewing up some really good coffee for the group. Some of the more exotic flavors such as Pumpkin Spice were originally scoffed at, but eventually, those same critics were some of our more consistent consumers. Pumpkin Spice now is a popular fall feature at Starbucks, so there! So, each afternoon, rotate who brews the coffee and bring it to each team member at their desk. Or if that is too much, simply provide those Keurig Green Mountain K-Cups for everyone and they can choose their own flavor.

- **Friday Bagels or Donuts** – this can either be done every Friday or at the end of each sprint, either way, it is something extra for the team to look forward to. In Texas, we actually did Friday *Breakfast Tacos* and that was a huge motivator. If you can do something like that or breakfast sandwiches, you have the team set through until lunch.
- **Sprint Planning Meeting Lunches** –for any long meetings such as the Sprint Planning meeting, please provide the common courtesy of having lunch provided. If the budget allows for it, this is a great thing to do each day for the project. If a Project Manager can take away the team's need to leave for an hour for food, the amount of productivity gained is far more than just that hour, and the effort is generally greatly appreciated. For me personally, taking away the need to find something for lunch is a great help every once in a while.
- **Evening-Work Late Dinners** – if the team is running behind towards the end of the sprint and needs to work late one night to catch up, by all means **provide dinner for them** during that time. Again, the costs of this will be made up by the increased productivity in this extra work time. Now, this should only be done *occasionally*, no need to do this on a daily basis or something has gone wrong with the sprint estimation. I worked this one project for a company which will remain nameless, a Swiss bank headquartered in Stamford, Connecticut. They had us working until 10 pm most nights, and never brought in dinner. The office cafeteria was not open, and by the time we left the office almost all area restaurants were closed. That was simply not right and not a good way to promote good team loyalty and performance. By

showing that they were not concerned with the well-being of the team members, several team members ultimately requested to be transferred to different projects.

- **End of Sprint/Milestone Happy Hours** – For each sprint or in the case of a Waterfall project, a major milestone completed, why not celebrate with a happy hour or a dinner?

CASE STUDY:

True Spirit Software And Energy Corporation
Building The Perfect Team:

So, we have already seen that Richard has a few problems to deal with in regards to his overall teams, but for now, he is simply focused in on creating the team for his first few Agile projects.

Thanks to Bill's help, Richard has identified Bhaskal as the technical resource to be used as a Scrum Master for the first two projects.

Also, since he realizes that Jim Ballenger has some major concerns about the new Agile plans, he has encouraged Jim to serve as Product Owner on the first two projects.

Now, would a Vice President of Trading normally be your Product Owner?

No.

But in this circumstance, Richard felt that it would help the overall process if Ballenger himself was more hands on. These two projects might then be more difficult and take longer, but the long term success would be far more likely if Ballenger was directly involved.

So for now, the team leaders are defined as:

Project Manager – Bill

Scrum Master – Bhaskal

Product Owner – Jim Ballenger

Bill is working with Jim to define the project initial set of requirements and once this is completed, Bill will draft the Project Charter and then define the remaining project team which will work under Bhaskal's supervision as Scrum Master.

The remaining project teams:

The team will utilize 3 Technical Leads which we have cross-trained as Scrum Masters. They will receive the full Agile Scrum Master training available nationwide. They will be able to help us with all agile projects and for Waterfall projects function as a technical lead.

Source of Staff:

For a shop of this size, we have sourced our staff using a combination of local workers, some outsourced developers, and some junior resources brought in for training, basic development, and then allowed to work towards the Project Management path.

Project Managers – local resources, all with PMP certifications and over 10 years PM experience

Junior PM – promoted from junior developer- came in on the junior developer program

Waterfall Developers – Indian-based outsourced team with our partner outsourcing company. We insist that they have a majority of their staff on site that rotate back to India periodically

Bill is working with Jim to define the project initial set of requirements and once this is completed, Bill will draft the Project Charter and then define the remaining project team which will work under Bhaskal's supervision as Scrum Master.

The remaining project teams:

The team will utilize 3 Technical Leads which we have cross-trained as Scrum Masters. They will receive the full Agile Scrum Master training available nationwide. They will be able to help us with all agile projects and for Waterfall projects function as a technical lead.

Source of Staff:

For a shop of this size, we have sourced our staff using a combination of local workers, some outsourced developers, and some junior resources brought in for training, basic development, and then allowed to work towards the Project Management path.

Project Managers – local resources, all with PMP certifications and over 10 years PM experience

Junior PM – promoted from junior developer- came in on the junior developer program

Waterfall Developers – Indian-based outsourced team with our partner outsourcing company. We insist that they have a majority of their staff on site that rotate back to India periodically

The five-hour time zone difference makes it realistic for the teams to work together for at least a half of a day and then coordinate all of their daily stand ups at a time that works for both teams.

In the meeting with the CIO, She rejects Richard's proposal for the six new off-shore resources, instead coming up with a compromise solution in which she will allow for three new offshore resources but she insists that Richard figure out a way to use the existing outsourced resources from India and the Philippines.

With this limitation, Richard works closely with Bill and Craig and finally builds out his project teams for the first two Agile projects.

The teams are as follows:

Team One:

Project Manager	**Bill**
Scrum Master	Bhaskal
Product Owner	Jim Ballenger
Team	Juanita
Team	Donna
Team	Kate
Team	Sam
Team	Gustavo(Chile)
Team	Corina(Chile)
Team	Almendra(Chile)

The way this will work is that Bill and Bhaskal will work together with Jim Ballenger to start the project off and then work with the remainder of the team once requirements are fleshed out.

Juanita will function as Technical Lead along with Bhaskal, who will continue to provide technical guidance as he operates in our modified vision of Scrum Master.

Gustavo and his Chile team will function inside the team but be given specific tasks each sprint to develop on their own since they are not located with the other team members. This is a known risk, and is less than ideal from an Agile perspective, but is a necessity.

Team Two:

Project Manager	**Craig**
Scrum Master	Shawn
Product Owner	Steve Bornstein
Team	Linda
Team	Andrew
Team	Dan
Team	DeSean
Team	Nerha(India)
Team	Ashnan(India)
Project Manager	Craig

This team is similar to the first team but is a little bit different. Craig will work with Shawn, who is another Technical Lead that they hope can transition to the role of Scrum Master.

Four of the developers, plus Shawn, will operate on site along with Nerha and Ashnan who will operate out of their remote office in India.

It has been agreed that all people, including offshore, will need to be available for the daily sprint meetings as well as the Sprint planning and Sprint retrospective meetings.

To take advantage of this time zone difference, Richard and Craig have decided to have all tasks developed by the on-site team, and then provide any QA and testing tasks to the offshore team, which will optimally result in basically almost a 24- hour development cycle if handled correctly.

The Product Owner for this project is another Vice President, at the same level as Jim Ballenger, by the name of Donald Bornstein. Mr. Bornstein heads the Software division and is very interested in the prospects of Agile development for reducing time to market, especially for minor enhancements but also for full version releases.

> After securing all of the commitments from the respective managers, Richard takes this list and presents it to Patty the CIO.
>
> Patty is pleased.
>
> On a less pleasant note, Richard had to inform Patty about Steve sabotaging the Agile conversion in the mind of the business users.
>
> Steve becomes the first casualty of the Agile conversion efforts as he is *terminated.*

DAILY
SPRINT
SPRINT
ITERATION
POTENTIALLY
SHIPPABLE
PRODUCT
SPRINT
BACKLOG
SPRINT
PLANNING
PRODUCT
BACKLOG

CHAPTER 9: Agile Project Management 2020

"You don't have to see the whole staircase, just take the first step"
-Martin Luther King, Jr.

For Agile Project Management 2020, the idea is not to reinvent Project Management or to create a new methodology. Our primary and core beliefs are that Agile is optimal for software development, Waterfall works best for several other project types, and that companies need to attempt to adopt Agile slowly and not rush in too quickly.

To summarize, Agile Project Management 2020 is an optimized evolution of Agile. We advocate an overarching strategy by which projects are managed due to their specific needs not because a certain methodology is hot at the moment.

We stress **communication** as being the A-1 and top focus of all Project Management skills.

Finally, we advocate using a Project Manager for all projects, and bring in Scrum Masters and Product Owners for Agile only projects. By doing this, we are always ready for any kind of project, whether they be Agile, Waterfall or some other methodology we don't even know about yet.

We have been asked the question many, many times before:

Which project management methodology should we use?

And as the good IT consultants that we are, our response is always the same non-committal but true response,

"It Depends"

This is not, however, as weak or indecisive of a response as it appears at first glance. The reason we respond this way is to concede the fact that the majority if not all of IT projects should be dictated by the specifics of the project requirements.

The key, as in the quote above, is to take action as early as possible. For example, if a project appears ready to go, and has a short timeline mandated, then assemble the team and get ready to go. Other times, specific, deliberate planning is required, and in those instances once this is analyzed, you still have made progress on the project.

One of the biggest mistakes that can be made very early on by a Project Manager is to assume or mandate the type of project management methodology to be used before considering the key specifics of that project.

Some projects just are not meant to be managed in an Agile manner. Some can be, but this type of analysis and observation is paramount when initiating a project. To make assumptions or just proceed blindly is a recipe for project disaster.

I worked with one Project Manager who was all excited and had just received his CSM (Certified Scrum Master) credential and was ready to apply this knowledge.

A project came in, and without really looking at the specifics in great detail, he did everything in his power to make it an Agile project, when the culture of the company and specifically the project sponsor, made it obvious to me that a Waterfall approach was called for.

Over my objections, he proceeded with the Agile approach which was a dismal failure and led to his ultimate departure from the company.

Remember this very simple, over used but still damn correct adage:

"The Customer Is Always Right"

Whether you agree with that statement or not, it ultimately is the case because the stakeholders have to agree whether a project is ultimately a success or a failure. Reality has no bearing here, it is simply stakeholder perception.

In our experience the determination of which project management methodology to use comes down to three key components:

1. The culture of the company
2. Personalities of the stakeholders
3. Availability of your project team

Company Culture:

As a PMO Manager or Project Manager, the culture of the company should already be quite familiar to you. This culture will greatly influence the project strategy and the viewpoints of the stakeholders.

It should come as no surprise, for example, that a bank would have multiple fixed date project requirements due to multiple reporting requirements and compliance issues. As a project manager on such a project, this needs to be factored in when considering your project management plan.

Conversely, a startup company or a web site, with no real fixed due dates mandated by reporting requirements may have significantly more flexibility. Again, this is not automatic, but a situation like this should come into the determination of your methodology.

As a project manager or a PMO Manager, it should be your job to evaluate your stakeholders, listen to what they are saying about the project and come to a conclusion about which methodology to use.

I would even advise being very open at the beginning of the project and telling the sponsor or key stakeholder what you are planning, and then gauge their response and go from there.

Stakeholder Personalities:

Many times the company culture will dictate the behavior of the stakeholders, as it impacts everything else. Still, with all sorts of disparate personality types it is important to know your audience and evaluate them to determine how to manage your project.

It would be easy to assume that a stakeholder for a banking project is still one who wants things done in a Waterfall methodology, only to find out later that this individual likes making last minute changes, is not a detailed planner and wants to be very involved on a daily basis. Conversely, you may determine that the owner of a startup has very fixed ideas on when deliverables should be provided and does not want any deviation from said plan.

Now personality evaluation is not an exact science. We are project managers here, not psychologists. All that we can realistically do is to speak with the stakeholders and project sponsors and do our **best** to gauge their personalities. Where possible also just simply speak to the other project managers and PMO Manager and get their take on how it is to work with this person.

Once you have interviewed these key people and really, really listened then you will have a really good idea of how to proceed with the project planning.

We also find this beneficial because the more you engage the sponsor and project stakeholders at the beginning, the more vested they become in the entire process, which will only help in the long run.

Personality Types: The Structured Organized, Planner:

We have worked with many project sponsors who are very detailed, time driven, and thorough. They want consistency, visibility and extensive forward planning. They do not like change, want a project to proceed in a linear fashion, and are a little confused by newer project methodologies and approaches.

Also, look for someone who wishes to be less involved with the project, if you determine that this person wants to just "fire and forget" you don't want to take the approach that requires significant involvement on their part.

If you couldn't already tell, for these individuals we recommend a more structured, Waterfall project management approach.

Personalities: The Indecisive, Borderline A.D.D Viewpoint:

On the other extreme is the indecisive sponsor who starts out a project with a great idea, but has precious few details that go along with that. The person is very bright, but has difficulty making hard and fast decisions. If this person appears willing to be very involved, and passionate then they are a candidate for an Agile project.

Now, we realize we have presented fairly extreme examples that are somewhat obvious. The truth is that there will likely be more grey area and judgment will need to be applied. The key point to remember as we stressed above:

"The Customer is Always Right"

As a project manager, it is critical to never mandate or make a unilateral decision on the project management methodology without considering company culture and personality of your sponsor and stakeholders. Ignore this advice at your own peril, trust us.

Project Team – Availability Issues:

The final factor that will dictate what type of project methodology to use is the availability and nature of the project team.

We make the suggestion that for Agile a project team has a minimum of 7 people active on any specific sprint, and then we like to have others available to rotate in to give others a periodic break.

If a project team is smaller than this, the team members are not available at the same time or there are other constraints, then plans must change.

Certain IT shops want to move to Agile because it is new, hip, and cool but their team members are not co-located nor are they available to work on the project at the same time.

Well not to be too simplistic, but this simply does not work. Without **most if not all** team members being available at the same time and located in the same place, Agile is less than ideal.

So, as a PMO Manager or Project Manager, analyze the available pool of talent and determine what can be done to structure your project(s) properly. For large shops with large teams this should work well because there is more flexibility.

For smaller shops where the work may need to be split out, Agile might not work since there are not enough available folks to be on a team. This all needs to be considered when planning the project methodology.

The Portfolio/PMO Manager:

In AgilePM2020, the role of the PMO Manager or Portfolio Manager is key, as we need to evaluate each project as it is formed and make some decisions how each project should be managed and what type of team to utilize.

How to Manage Different Types of Projects:

Here is a sample description of some project ideas, see if you can identify the recommended Project Management methodology to apply.

Sample Portfolio Project 1: Server Upgrade

This project features the upgrade of 6 physical servers along with adding some virtual servers. Much of the specific details are not yet known, but what is known is the limitation of the ordering cycle, that will take between 4-6 weeks.

Sample Portfolio Project 2: Software Patch

This project involves the structured and scheduled deployment of a software patch across 200 machines.

Sample Portfolio Project 3: New Web Site Development

A company has the framework and some basic story boards done on a few web pages for the site. Much of the remaining functionality still needs to be defined.

Sample Portfolio Project 4: Script Modifications

Scripts which are normally maintained by the offshore team, need significant modifications. The requirements are known, and the planned duration is approximately two weeks.

Sample Portfolio Project 5: Third Party Software Purchase, Implementation and Custom Interfaces and Configurations

This project involves evaluating multiple vendors and their products, the purchase of said product and implementation across the enterprise.

The project will involve six interfaces to in-house legacy applications, much of the details of which are not yet known.

In addition, the software will need to be custom configured to meet the needs of the business.

See Appendix 2 For Our Recommendations

CASE STUDY:

True Spirit Software and Energy Corporation

The projects that Richard has elected to start with are all projects that are fairly obvious candidates for Agile.

The projects selected are a new fuel scheduling desktop application and a new web landing page to be used as a tie in to a Google Adwords campaign for the software.

The fuel scheduling tool is only for internal users, whereas the web page and Adwords campaign is designed for universal use.

Patty is frustrated to learn that not all projects in the pipeline have been evaluated as being Agile candidates.

"Your direction was simple, Richard." Patty says with anger, "I want all projects to be managed using Agile by the end of the year."

"I understand, Patty, but we just don't have the required teams." Richard replies.

"Well, we need to get the teams then. I want my orders implemented, or it will be on **you** if they are not." Patty sternly replies.

Richard pauses for a moment, so that he can think of a more diplomatic response than the profanity-laden response he is considering, but knows will be a career-limiting move.

"Patty, wasn't it in fact, you, who told me that I could only bring on half of the resources that I requested."

Patty does not respond, but only reluctantly nods.

"It was you that imposed the budgetary limits, and now you want all of the projects to be managed with Agile, which is a great idea. It's a great idea, but for this year and with our current budget constraints, we simply cannot handle right now."

"But if you had the necessary budget, **then** you could implement Agile? Correct?" Patty persists.

Richard realizes that no amount of debate is going to sway her from her set position, so he relents, knowing that the budget issues will always be there.

"Right," Richard says, "if we had the available budget, then we should be able to run all projects in an Agile manner."

Richard grits his teeth as he exits from Patty's office.

He knows it is unlikely that there will ever be enough money to run all projects with agile, but fears that if there is, then he must ultimately have another showdown with Patty.

It's a showdown that he is very unlikely to win.

CHAPTER 10: Getting Your Company To Evolve Slowly

"The "P" in Project Management is as much about "people management" as it is about "project management"
--Cornelius Fichtner

Again, a theme in this book that repeats and repeats is the simple fact that Project Management does not succeed without good people management.

This means the project teams, the IT managers and more importantly the business and/or customers.

One of the biggest mistakes that we have seen companies make is to commit to a methodology and overwhelm the business. By making sudden and dramatic changes, it serves to create a backlash against what otherwise very well have been successful efforts.

The principles of gradualism

There is a scientific principle that applies to the corporate adoption of Agile methodologies that is called **gradualism.**

Gradualism is a theory or a tenet assuming that change comes about gradually or that variation is gradual in nature

In our experience and observations, one major reason that Agile fails at companies is due to the fact that the companies implement it unilaterally, too quickly, and then either the business or IT revolts against its implementation.

Then, a company has one of two options: Either stick with a losing methodology, or push forward and mandate it over the objections of both the business and IT.

First, a very simple point: *If the business does not approve of what project management processes that are being used, then it needs to stop.* IT shops that serve internal business units should never attempt to drive a methodology over a business objection that is simply not the way that it works.

I heard the story of a CIO who was so committed to a certain type of software that he purchased it without clearing it with the business, and was ultimately fired.

So, all of this is said to prove a basic point which repeats as a recurring theme in this book. The rule should be to implement Agile where it is **appropriate** and only when the business fully "buys in" to the operation.

This is simple human nature at work. How many of us, especially as we are older and more entrenched in our careers would welcome a swift and complete process change in our daily lives?

If you answered "yes", then more power to you, but I think for the majority of us out there change is perceived with suspicion and resistance and its full benefits are only recognized over time.

Companies many times want to go completely Agile and do it all at once because some Director read an Agile book or went to some training class and it needs to be remembered that people in general are always reluctant to change.

Implement this slowly and demonstrate the benefits to the business and the IT team. Gradually define roles and explain to individuals the opportunity to grow their skills and expand their visibility in the enterprise. Provide the opportunity to get training and certification options, but only a few people at a time, say for the first planned Agile team.

For the existing Project Managers, explain that their roles are not being eliminated, but rather changing to be more dynamic. It is a great idea to provide Agile training opportunities for these project managers as well.

Put a plan in place that will enable a one year or eighteen month transition period to either going full Agile, or as is recommended in this book, the hybrid Agile Project Management 2020 approach which allows for both Agile and Waterfall based on the project and based on the specifics of the business needs.

On the next few pages we will provide specific examples on how to build and become an Agile or Agile PM 2020 shop over an 12 month period.

The Agile Project Management 2020 Implementation Plan:

Month One	Meet with IT managers and key business managers and discuss the planned change and how it will be handled on a project by project basis and phased in gradually
Month Two:	Discuss this idea with the Project Management team. Explain the opportunities to learn Agile and that the role of the Project Manager is changing, but not going away
Month Three:	Start planning the initial Agile team. Identify 2-3 Scrum Masters from the existing technical team and maybe one current Project Manager who wants to learn Scrum
Month Four:	Schedule Agile training and certified Scrum master programs for the identified Scrum Masters. This training is only 2-3 days so for the initial Agile team of 7-9 should not be all that expensive

Month Five:	Meet with business to identify Process Owners. Discuss projects that might be good candidates for Agile.
Month Six:	Take the pilot Agile project and identify all of the team members, including Project Manager, Process Owner and Scrum Master
Month Seven:	Meetings set up to draft the Project Charter and project plan and then the overall Sprint project plan. This plan will be to define the number of sprints, not the specifics of each sprint
Month Eight:	First sprints begin
Month Nine:	First project in progress; begin second project following the plan noted above
Month Ten:	First project in progress; second project getting team developed
Month Eleven:	First project in progress; second project planning meetings
Month Twelve:	First project completed; second project first sprint started.

So, what do we end up with here? We have one project completed and another one underway. We also have two developed Agile teams and an informed user base. As these projects are occurring, other projects are being managed in the standard Waterfall methodology with very little impact to the business.

Notice that for the second project, the amount of lead time was significantly reduced, as a great deal of what was needed had already been mapped out from the first Agile project. For this reason, we highly recommend a slow and methodical approach be taken for the first Agile project to not rush the business and also overwhelm the IT people.

And as the initial shock of this change wears off, the second and subsequent projects generally go much faster as anything once the initial learning curve is covered.

Remember, as a rule, people can be resistance to change. With that in mind, if the idea is to make long-term and lasting change, then implement it gradually. Do not rush just to sooth some need to be current or do what other companies are doing. Manage the business and the IT people like you want a gradual and sustained change, don't push something on them that they might rebel against it simply because of the rapid nature of the change.

In this way, for Agile Project Management 2020, we advise implementing this change gradually, really understand the specific needs of each project, and keeping an open mind in regards to methodology.

It is too easy to just make a blanket statement and/or take the same strategy for all projects. Just like trying to make one diet for all people, this rarely if ever works.

We feel that Agile Project Management 2020 is the preferred strategy to bringing Agile to an organization. It is designed to work **with** existing PMO's and not attempt to reinvent the proverbial wheel.

We know in theory that going "all Agile" or "all Waterfall" is an easier, and maybe even more appealing alternative. We also know that this approach misses out on opportunities to do the most appropriate and correct thing for your business.

Also, in a pragmatic sense, Agile Project Management 2020 works better because you have retained your existing Project Management team and made existing technical people Scrum Masters. If something happens, and management dictates a return to all Waterfall methodologies, then people are in the correct roles and no changes are required.

If, on the other hand, a company goes all Agile and replaces Project Managers with Scrum Masters, what can be done then once a company decides to return to Waterfall?

If yours is a company that has read about Agile and want to consider it, we highly recommend this more phased and structured Agile Project Management 2020 approach as opposed to a blanket and sudden paradigm shift.

CASE STUDY:

True Spirit Software and Energy Corporation

Almost a year later, the first two Agile projects are widely considered to be a success.

Jim Ballenger, initially one of the biggest opponents of the implementation of Agile, is now one of its biggest champions.

Ballenger has identified the fact that new projects are quicker, and more importantly, contain more of the features that the business actually needs NOW as opposed to something that was planned six months prior, and is no longer a major priority.

Bornstein also agrees that it has been a success, especially for his software division. Now, teams are able to get software updates done every other week, and the entire process just has everyone far more content than before.

Fresh off this success, and more than happy to take the credit, CIO Patty Smith moves to further implement her mandate and demands that all remaining projects be converted to Agile.

In a IT CIO meeting with the PMO Manager and the Directors, she reiterates her mandate over the strong objections of the PMO Manager Richard and the other Directors.

"For our server upgrade projects we simply cannot use Agile." Andrew the Director of Infrastructure says.

"I agree," Richard says. "Besides, I thought we discussed this, and there simply was not the necessary budget to complete this."

Rob, a senior Director, and the man that likely would have become CIO had the company not decided to seek an external hire, speaks up.

"I have looked at the budget numbers, Patty, and we have no additional budget for training, new outsourced or any other new team members." Rob says.

Patty shows a look on her face such that she is not wanting to debate at the moment.

"Will all of you just do as you are told, please?" Patty barks.

Monique, director of Networking, decides to speak up as well, in her heavy French accent.

"I am afraid that I have to agree with the gentlemen, madam. Lest you feel that it is all the men ganging up on you because you are a woman."

"Nobody thought that." Patty says dismissively. "Listen, I appreciate all of your opinions, but that does not mean that I need to listen to them. I am the CIO here, and I expect all of you to listen to me. Don't worry about the budget, I know what I can do to make the numbers work."

Patty dismisses the meeting and the other directors get together along with Richard to discuss their concerns.

Unknown to Patty, Rob is very close to the Chief Financial Officer and Rob warns the CFO to monitor Patty's spending closely.

Within three months, multiple unauthorized transactions are flagged and brought to the CFO's attention.

A few months after that, Patty Smith is reassigned to another department in the company, and is demoted from her C-level position to that of Senior Director.

Does this scenario seem far-fetched to you?

This exact and specific scenario is fiction, but it is based on stories and observations in which very similar fates were met by individuals who felt like they were insulated and protected by their positions.

We have seen CIOs, directors, managers, project managers and others all fail and get terminated due to behavior like this. The lack of flexibility, and more importantly lack of listening to other viewpoints can be career killers regardless of what level your position is.

We also wanted to put that part in for all of you who have had bad bosses or co-workers that you **hoped** would meet a similar career fate. Trust me, bad behavior is ultimately caught, it just sometimes takes longer than all of us "good guys" would like.

The key mistake that Patty made in this example was rushing the change, and not listening to the people who were closer to the day to day operations.

David B. Twilley, PMP, CSM

> Whether it is a programming language, ERP system, or project management methodology, ultimately these are simply tools. To ignore the needs and opinions of your team because you are just committed to a certain tool just simply makes no sense. It is fine to have a preference, a bias based on experience but that should not blind one to new opportunities.

CHAPTER 11: Putting It All Together

> Okay, so now there is a consensus in the organization that agile project management methodolgies should be combined with Waterfall and each project evaluated on its own merits.
>
> The logical next question is: "What now?"
>
> In this section, it will be all case study to evaluate exactly how agile and waterfall would blend together in the first few months, and to pay particular attention to the first few agile projects.
>
> This is not a standard instructional chapter, rather this is the real-world from the beginning step-by-step guide of what the Agile Project Management 2020 project pipeline would look like.
>
> We have already covered the project pipeline review steps, and the team selection and steps such as that, but what then?

Now, let's look at the overall view of a complete process implementing all of the concepts of AgilePM2020.

This will include the following:

PMO Project Pipeline review

Richard will meet and discuss projects in the queue and sort out which will be addressed in the short term

Project Selection

Two projects selected – one will be handled by Mark as Waterfall, and one by Bill as AgilePM2020 with

Bhaskal as Scrum Maste

Of the two projects selected – one will be handled by Mark as Waterfall, and one by Bill as AgilePM2020 with Bhaskal as Scrum Master

PROJECT PHASES --- HOW WILL THE PROJECT BE HANDLED DIFFERENTLY

INITIATION:

So, for both projects, the Agile and the Waterfall project, the Project Manager will draft the Project Charter.

This document will formally establish the project and provide audit compliance.

Mark completes his Project Charter for the Waterfall project.

Bill completes the Project Charter for the Agile project, NOT Bhaskal the Scrum Master.

PLANNING:

The planning stage will be significantly different for both projects. Mark will spend several weeks to a month gathering detailed requirements, building a project scope statement, and creating a detailed project plan.

Bill will work with Product Owner Jim Ballenger and a little with Bhaskal the Scrum Master to craft an overview of the project timeline, set budget information, and get a very high level list of requirements.

This planning phase still has to exist, and in our vision of responsibilities, the Project Manager is very involved in this component

EXECUTION:

It is in the execution phase that the paths of our Project Managers will deviate greatly based on whether the project is Agile or Waterfall.

For Mark's waterfall project, he will conduct weekly status meetings, update gantt chart with progress, request and receive status report updates and be more of a authoritarian leader.

For Bill, most of his work is done, but at the start of the project, he will introduce the Scrum Master and then turn the operation of the Scrums over to the Scrum Master.

Bill can add value by continuing to liaise with the business and providing communication to other groups, such that the Scrum Master does not need to do this.

First Agile Project -- Now that the first project has started, let's look at our first Agile Project Management 2020 project team:

Team One:

Project Manager	**Bill**
Scrum Master	Bhaskal
Product Owner	Jim Ballenger
Team	Juanita
Team	Donna
Team	Kate
Team	Sam
Team	Gustavo(Chile)
Team	Corina(Chile)
Team	Almendra(Chile)
QA Team(India)	Nerha
QA Team(India)	Ashnan

Note that the primary project team is the top 7 individuals, the final two will be utilized to augment the primary project team and provide QA for that near round-the-clock development cycle that Patty and Richard alluded

Project One: Energy Hedge Software Modification

This project is one of Jim Ballenger's priorities; it will accomplish two main objectives along with some minor feature enhancements. The initial plan is to make the modifications for the internal trading team, and then after all of those requirements have been completed to then make the modifications available to the software customers.

For now, Jim Ballenger acts as Product Owner and is working with his team to develop the Product Backlog.

In parallel to this, Richard has worked with Bill to develop the Project Charter and the Preliminary Project Scope statement.

Working on a third path, Bhaskal and Bill discuss the basics of how they will work together and what the lines of demarcation might be.

It is an awkward conversation at first.

"I don't understand," Bhaskal says, "I thought that Agile teams don't need managing, that the team is *self-managing*."

"Well, that is mostly true," Bill replies, "what we are doing here is that I will help form the initial structure of the project, get the audit documents done such as the project charter."

"Okay, yes I guess I would not want to do that." Bhaskal says.

"Right," Bill responds, "and then once we get the project off the ground, the charter and scope statement is completed, I will then turn the project over to you and the Product Owner to run the day to day."

Bhaskal nods and appears to understand.

"I see," Bhaskal responds, "so at that point, it will be the agile team that will self manage, no project manager checking on status and things of that nature."

"Exactly," Richard replies "think of it this way. The Project Manager will help structure the project, help frame it, whereas the product owner and the team **itself** will be responsible for the execution and completion of it."

So, Bill and Bhaskal define how they plan to work together, which hopefully will set the framework for future projects.

In the meantime, Jim Ballenger has completed his meetings with his team and they have come back with a list of 30 product backlog items.

Ballenger and his team have also prioritized all of the product backlog items and put them in prioritized order.

Now, they are ready to have a planning session to scope out the sprints for the project.

Jim Ballenger, Richard, Bill, Bhaskal and the Project Team get together in the largest conference room available. Bill and Jim set up the meeting by providing breakfast foods and also schedule lunch for later that day. The assumption is that this could take all day to complete.

Richard negotiated with the CIO to fly the Chile-based outsourced team in as well since they will be part of the non-QA project team. For each future sprint planning meeting, they will participate via teleconference.

Bill introduces Jim to the others on the team, especially Bhaskal, and explains what the roles and interactions will be and the weekly sprint schedule.

Jim asks several questions and Richard is there to help with explaining the specifics of how everything will work between the teams.

"So, Bhaskal will be my daily contact, since he is the so-called Scrum Master?" Ballenger asks.

"Exactly," Richard says, "Bill is here to help, but once the project gets going, let's use Bhaskal as your day to day leader."

Bhaskal nods, quietly wondering how this might work considering he is fairly tranquil, and Jim Ballenger has a, let's just say, bombastic personality to say the least.

Richard then instructs Jim to start the demonstration, and begins walking through a slideshow upon which on each slide he and his team have defined User Stories, a.k.a Requirements, for each requested piece of functionality.

After walking through and explaining the first slide, Jim asks Bhaskal almost confrontationally, "so how long do you think this would take?"

Bhaskal looks surprised by this question and does not respond. Richard steps in and bails Bhaskal out.

"For this, Jim, we actually expect the entire team to participate in the estimation process." Richard says.

"Why is that? " Ballenger contends, "If **he** is the authority why wouldn't he do the estimating?"

"That's one of the points of Agile, Jim." Richard says, "It is all about the team. The team estimates, the team delivers, the team functions together, not like traditional Waterfall with a PM estimating and then driving tasks.

"Okay, I guess, "Jim says, now turning to face the other team members, "So, I will ask the entire team, how long do you think it will take to complete this task?"

This time Bill steps in to answer, "Actually, Jim, what we want to do here is to let each of the team members write down a number that will weight each of these tasks by **proportional effort**, and then we will compare and average all of the numbers."

"Proportional effort? You mean *hours*, right?" Ballenger asks.

"No, not hours," Richard intercedes, "but level of effort. This way tasks are more relative, compared to each other. It will take a few iterations for us to determine how this weighting then equates to hours."

Ballenger does not look convinced.

"Fine, whatever, so let's just get a number going." Ballenger says.

"In front of each of you," Richard starts, "there are about 50 blank pieces of paper and a marker. For each of these user stories, please write a number that is indicative of the relative effort. Numbers that we want to use are 1, 2, 5, 8, 13, 21. For now, let's just rank them like this, and we can refine this as we go along."

"Why set numbers like 1,2, 5 etc?" Gustavo asks, "Why can't we just set a value as we see it?"

"That's a good question, Gustavo." Richard responds, "the reason for this is that we are just trying to get a rough order of magnitude estimate, or ROM, and something that we can compare each task to as a group."

The team members look at each other curiously, but ultimately nod in understanding and proceed to follow the instructions.

So, for the next few hours, Ballenger completes his list of the user stories and the team follows instructions ranking each task by relative effort.

At the end of the user story review session, Richard has all of the team members return all of the user stories to Bill and Bhaskal, who will process each and then come up with an average rating for each user story.

Richard has the team break for lunch, and then gives Bill and Bhaskal a few hours to average out the estimates for each story.

When the team members return, they all take their seats and then Bill and Bhaskal approach Jim Ballenger to discuss the finding and begin reviewing the possibilities for

the first sprint. Ballenger requests that only the top five requests be reviewed to start.

Bhaskal and Bill present the user stories in sequential order based on the priority that Ballenger as Product Owner established them.

The first two tasks are fairly straightforward and feature a consensus number of 2. Ballenger agrees with this and the team moves on to discuss item number 3, which has a weighting of 21.

"21?" Ballenger exclaims, "That is ridiculous, this one task cannot take that long."

Richard interjects, "What is full description of this story, Bill?"

"This is the hedge management screen that will involve changes to all three tiers, including significant database changes." Bill answers.

"We estimated that a single developer would need about three months to complete this." Bhaskal adds.

"But working in a focused manner, the team expects to complete it within two weeks." Richard adds.

"That still seems like a high estimate to me, but I will trust you guys this time." Ballenger concedes, reluctantly.

Bill looks up and motions towards Richard, "We have reached our initial velocity target of 25 story points, did we want to continue to review the others?"

Richard looks at Ballenger, "Jim, did you want to review the others, or can that wait until the next sprint meeting?"

Ballenger hesitates and then adds, "Ideally, we would review them all, but if your team is comfortable with this, and if you are telling me I can have that hedge management screen in two weeks, then I am happy."

Richard looks down at his phone to check the time and then adds, "Tell you what, since we are a few hours ahead of schedule, why don't we go ahead and look at the next few."

Ballenger nods and then adds, "Okay, but just a few more."

Bill and Bhaskal continue with the list and they mark the following entries and the corresponding story points:

Priority	Name	Description	Story Points
4	VAR	New value at risk calculation and screen	21
5	Real Time Quotes	New Real Time quotes screen – quote data is already there	11
6	Custom Hedge Report	Report that shows position of hedges and evaluates	21
7	Modify Profit and Loss Report	Add two columns to existing reports	5

This and the remaining items will remain on the Product Backlog, while the items selected for the current sprint will be considered to be

SPRINT BACKLOG (SPRINT 1)

So, the product backlog review is considered to be completed, and the sprint backlog is set with the following items: This means that these three items will be completed (or attempted) during the two-week sprint based on their initial *goal velocity* of 25.

Priority	Name	Description	Story Points
1	Modification Executive Dashboard – New Drill	Add a drill to existing executive dashboard	2
2	Executive Dashboard – add users	Set security such that Super User can have admin rights	2
3	Hedge Management Screen	Screen that evaluates and notifies based on hedge conditions	21

The Sprint Meeting And Daily Stand-Up

At the designated starting date for the first sprint, the team gathers to discuss the plan for the first day of the first sprint.

Richard has procured a white board and the necessary color-coded sticky notes and worked with Bhaskal and Bill to draw the appropriate columns.

In the To-Do column they have placed just the sprint backlog items, the items that the team has agreed to work on for this two-week sprint.

At this point, the other items on the product backlog are irrelevant, as they have been specifically omitted from this sprint, therefore they are not a part of the short term plan.

The group gathers in a central and open area and all sit around a large table. Bhaskal stands with Bill at the front of the room by the board and are flanked to their right by the Product Owner, Jim Ballenger.

Bill is there primarily to observe and serve as liaison for Ballenger until he becomes comfortable with the new process, but Bhaskal plans to lead this meeting.

"The team and I have discussed this," Bhaskal begins, "and the decision was that we should focus on the hedge management screen, the more difficult task, and do that first."

"Wait," Ballenger responds, "I thought we had that as third on our list."

"We did, sir," Bhaskal says, "but we felt that this would be a great item to start on that would help build our team effort. The other tasks are more of a one or two person task."

Ballenger nods his head, "Okay, go on."

"Well, that is really it, sir." Bhaskal responds, "since that is the big-ticket item, we will begin on this today and we will provide further updates in tomorrow's meeting."

"And that's it?" Ballenger asks.

"Yes, that's it." Bhaskal responds.

Ballenger smiles as he begins to get up from his chair, "Wow, that is the best meeting that I have ever been to."

The group laughs lightly, and everyone gets back to work.

Remaining Daily Stand-Up Sprint Meetings During First Sprint:

Nothing especially interesting happens in the next several sprint meetings, as the focus is on reporting progress on only the one agreed upon task for the sprint backlog.

On the final day of the sprint things become a little more interesting, and some of the good and the bad of the Agile strategy are revealed.

Bhaskal continues to lead the daily stand up sprint meetings and is leading the final day of the sprint, which is the Friday of the second week. It was agreed that the team would do the final sprint meeting and then defer the sprint retrospective until the following Monday.

"So, we have completed the hedge tracking screen, which was our large item for this sprint," Bhaskal says, "the India team is in final stages of QA right now, and we have a few minor changes that our Chile team expects to have finished by Noon our time today."

"That means we are totally finished, right?" Ballenger asks.

"Well, not entirely," Bhaskal responds, "we have finished, or *will finish*, this task since it was our primary focus, but the other two items are still iffy."

"What does that mean, exactly?" Ballenger asks.

Richard sees the opportunity to make some clarifying points.

"It means one of two things, Jim," Richard says, "We either finish these report changes today and roll it out this weekend, or it gets pushed back to the next sprint."

Ballenger hesitates but does not respond.

"Most likely," Bhaskal continues, "we will complete one, but not both of the requests."

"So, all that means is that it goes back into the list for completion later, is that right?" Ballenger asks.

"Exactly, we will do it, it just won't make it in this release, that is all."

"I can live with that," Ballenger responds, "I am quite pleased that you guys finished the hedge tracking system so fast, seriously, the middle office guys are going to love this."

"Are the other team members responding well to the new agile strategy?" Bhaskal asks.

"Are you kidding me?" Ballenger responds with a smile, "the way those guys look at it, is that we can be wrong with our requirements **twice a month** and still turn out okay."

"I have heard from several in your team that they especially like not having to wait months at a time for what they perceive as fairly simple functionality." Richard adds.

"What we **really** like, Richard, is the opportunity to change our minds frequently, and not have what is known as 'sunk cost' affect us adversely." Ballenger says.

"That's why I thought your team would love it." Richard says as he nods.

The First Sprint Retrospective

Friday night, the code for the first sprint is deployed into production and the first sprint is considered completed.

Utilizing the multiple-team time zone advantages, Bhaskal has the India QA run some final tests first thing Monday morning, and then also has the Chilean team review for a few hours just to be doubly sure

First thing Monday morning on the West Coast, the team gathers first for the sprint retrospective meeting.

This meeting is held in an actual conference room away from distractions, and only including the project team members.

The Chile team is not physically there, but has dialed in, along with the India QA team, even though the meeting is not at a very convenient time for them.

Richard makes the introductions, and then turns it over to Bhaskal to continue the discussion.

"Overall," Bhaskal begins, "this was a very successful first sprint. To summarize, we were able to complete the large hedge function and one of the additional requirements to give us a total velocity of 23. The hedge item had a weighting of 21 and the report modification only had a weighting of 2."

"Velocity?" Ballenger asks, sarcastically, "what, are we driving a `car` here?"

The crowd laughs lightly and Richard interjects, "Yeah, I never understood why they used that term, but in this context velocity refers to the volume or rate of work accomplished in a sprint."

"Oh yeah," Ballenger says, "Was that the number that was originally set as 25?"

"Right," Bhaskal says, "but that was before our first sprint, and now we know about the right velocity for this team, we will reset this number to 23."

"And what purpose does that serve?" Ballenger asks.

"Well now," Richard says, "now, when we plan our sprints, instead of planning for 25 and missing, we target 23 and then keep adjusting the number as we have more sprints."

"I get it," Ballenger responds, "and then after multiple sprints, you can adjust it accordingly sort of like a moving average of the sprints."

Bhaskal continues to discuss the first sprint, and notes how the first week had some issues with communication with the Chile team, but for the second week it got a lot better.

The Chile team has agreed to have one rotating team member that works the U.S schedule, and the other two will continue to work their normal schedule which is five hours ahead of the west coast based corporate office.

The India-based QA team is viewed as being a big success. Bhaskal was responsible for setting up the process to pass of the developed code each day to the two offshore QA resources and then for them to forward to the Chile team and then ultimately back to the U.S team. There was a problem one day with communication. But for a first sprint, to only have a 10% problem with so many potential disconnect points, was viewed as a success.

Second Sprint Planning Meeting:

Now, it is time for the second sprint planning meeting, which the team has decided to have on the same day as the Sprint Retrospective.

Since they are consuming this first day of what would be the second sprint, they have agreed to reduce the targeted Velocity from the new number of 23 down to 21 to compensate for an approximate 10% loss in available time.

As these sprints progress, there should ideally be less time consumed by such meetings.

Ballenger Presents Product Backlog

Jim Ballenger, the Product Owner, takes center stage and begins to present the new prioritized product backlog.

The one item that was not completed in the previous sprint has been added back to the product backlog, and the priorities have been reset.

Here was the remaining Product Backlog **before** the first sprint:

Priority	Name	Description	Story Points
4	VAR	New value at risk calculation and screen	21
5	Real Time Quotes	New Real Time quotes screen – quote data is already there	11
6	Custom Hedge Report	Report that shows position of hedges and evaluates	21
7	Modify Profit and Loss Report	Add two columns to existing reports	5

After the first sprint, there was a remaining undelivered backlog item, so it was added back to the product backlog.

In addition, during that two week sprint, Ballenger met with his team and re-prioritized their list, which ultimately led to one of the items being **completely removed** from the list.

Now, this is one of the big benefits of Agile right here. Rather than working from a static list of old requirements, the project team is always working on the most current

David B. Twilley, PMP, CSM

> Is it likely that something be dropped so soon in the project? No, probably not, but what does happen is that going into the fourth or fifth sprints, those seemingly important requirements tend to drop off very quickly as the business really thinks about and analyzes their need.
>
> Here is the revised near-term Product Backlog once a few adjustments have been made:

The Agile Project Manager 2020

Priority	Name	Description	Story Points
REMOVED	VAR	New value at risk calculation and screen	21
4	Real Time Quotes	New Real Time quotes screen – quote data is already there	11
5	Modification Executive Dashboard – New Drill	Carried over from the first sprint	2
6	Custom Hedge Report	Report that shows position of hedges and evaluates	21
7	Modify Profit and Loss Report	Add two columns to existing reports	5
8	Financial Trade Analysis Report	Revision to existing Financial Trade report	3

Notice how the first item has been removed, and item number 5 is the carryover item from the first sprint.

To stick to the planned velocity of 21 story points, the team views the list and selects all of the near-term items except item #6 which is 21 story points all by itself.

The decision is made to, at least for now, push that item to the third sprint.

This cycle continues until the project is considered to be complete by the business. What typically happens when things go well is that the business ends the project once they get their big ticket deliverables as they really are not all that concerned about the "nice to have" items.

CHAPTER 12: Conclusion

"Ability is what you are capable of doing. Motivation determines what you do. Attitude determines how well you do it."
--Lou Holtz

It is very important for companies to have a dynamic and realistic strategy when it comes to managing projects.

It should not be a simple blanket decision when evaluating each project to summarize it and say "We are an Agile shop, so we are running this project with Agile".

Project Management is all about communication, and if this communication with the stakeholders indicates that Agile will not work, and then do not **force it.**

The role of the traditional Project Manager should **not go away.** As companies rush to go Agile, this seems like an easy win, one less position to keep. This is an oversimplification and a mistake.

The role of the Project Manager is still needed, but the role simply needs to be handled a little bit differently than in previous years.

Management needs to adapt and Project Managers need to adapt

Management needs to:

- Listen and evaluate each project
- Help project managers build their skills

Project Managers must:

- *Understand the boundaries* – for Agile projects, they need to not interfere when the Scrum Master is coordinating the work
- *Become more technical* – I don't see any place for the non-technical project manager in software development. For some of the longer-tenured non-technical Project Managers, this might not work out. For the younger group, provide them some basic technical training as part of their development plan.
- *Improve their Communication* – with the AgilePM2020 model, we have freed up the time of the Project Manager to communicate that much more often, and hopefully that much more effectively than ever before.

We think that by having a solid team that communicates well that the result is a very solid project team. An organization should be ready to manage projects based upon the unique needs of the project itself, not because of some mandated methodology or "flavor of the month"

Applying the basic concepts of Agile Project Management 2020, we feel that your enterprise will be well prepared to handle any type of project that comes up. You will also have a more well-developed and diverse team which will result in more content stakeholders. And a happy customer is typically a repeat customer.

The Agile Project Manager 2020

For more information, please visit us at www.true-spiritconsulting.com to learn more about Agile Project Management 2020.

Thanks for reading this book and good luck with all of your projects.

David B. Twilley, PMP, CSM, Six Sigma Green Belt

David.Twilley@True-SpiritConsulting.com

David B. Twilley, PMP, CSM

CASE STUDY:

True Spirit Software and Energy Corporation

Now that Patty Smith has been reassigned, Rob has been appointed as the interim CIO.

The first agile projects have been considered successes and the business is very pleased with the quick turnaround on their requests.

Thanks to solid support from Agile champions, Mr. Ballenger and Bornstein, the Agile plan will continue for all projects in which it is deemed appropriate.

Rob has provided the PMO Manager Richard full discretion to determine the Project Management methodology for all projects.

With this discretion, Richard has set up monthly meetings with his Project Managers in which they evaluate all new Project proposals and sort them based on priority, difficult and benefit. When they do this, they also identify the optimal Project Management methodology.

With the current pace, by the end of the second year Agile should be well-accepted and implemented throughout the organization.

Simple and finite projects will continue to be managed using traditional Waterfall methodology, but the majority of software and development projects will be managed with Agile.

APPENDIX 1: "Running The Perfect Meeting"

How many times have we endured a meeting that we simply should not have been invited to?

More than a few, I am sure.

The idea for the modern meeting should be to have a focused purpose, correct audience, and an agenda which should be maintained throughout the duration of the meeting.

I believe that one of the benefits of taking the Agile approach is that there ideally should be fewer meetings required. This is the case because with an Agile team working together, they should be collaborating and sharing information the entire way, without the need to get everyone together, since they are **already** together.

But, especially early on in the planning and initiation phases, these types of larger group meetings are unavoidable, so we would like to discuss some observations, tips and tricks for optimizing your project meetings.

Here is a list of some of the key points we will discuss in regards to optimizing project meetings:

1. Specified Meeting Agenda -- For each meeting, in the meeting email include an initial agenda and a few line items about what is to be discussed
2. Recurring Meetings -- If this is a recurring meeting, send an update at least 30 minutes before including the revised agenda. For a recurrence, it is safe to assume that the discussion will vary each week so handle that accordingly
3. Invite the correct people. This is more art than science, but it is imperative that the correct audience is included for the correct meeting.
4. Optimize roll call. Take roll call at once, rather than identifying people as they dial in.
5. Control the meeting conversations. If a sidebar conversation goes five minutes or more politely re-purpose the conversation and note that the conversation should be resumed "offline".
6. Meeting minutes. Provide some basic communication as to what was covered. An important output from these meeting minutes would be Action items which are nothing more than some quick bullet items so it is clear to all in attendance what the next steps are and more importantly who is responsible.

The Meeting Agenda:

All meetings and especially recurring meetings need to have a scheduled and planned agenda. I know that I have fallen into this trap in regards to recurring meetings, where my only agenda is "recurring scheduled meeting" and this was a big mistake.

Meetings such as these should be *evaluated* and their value determined, and if there is no value then the Project Manager should consider canceling them, but by carefully explaining to the audience why the meeting has been canceled.

Back to the agenda, so the day of the meeting, plan it out and then update the Outlook meeting notification with a two to five line summary of agenda.

This does a few things for you. First, it serves as an active meeting reminder, telling the attendees that the meeting is still one. Secondly, it serves as talking points, to keep the meeting on topic and hopefully avoid unnecessary sidebar conversations. And finally, it serves as a starting point for the documentation of meeting minutes, and something to review for those unable to attend the meeting.

As far as the timing of this update, by all means send this update a minimum of a half hour before the meeting is scheduled. I recall at one of my projects, the PM would send an update five minutes before the meeting, but most of the attendees were already on their way to the conference room, and therefore, would not have the agenda. She did this every week without fail, and several team members complained about it.

What I typically do is to send the update with the meeting agenda about an hour before the meeting and that seems to please most people.

Inviting the Correct People:

Now this one is more art than science, but we have learned that it is absolutely imperative to invite the correct audience for each meeting, and not just invite everybody that you can think of.

The goal of most project meetings should be to generate an outcome, come to a consensus, basically to get something DONE. The more people involved in a meeting, the more distracted and detached most participants become, especially if the meeting is a conference call meeting.

Our Meeting Guidelines.
Meeting Type and the appropriate audiences:

Meeting Type	Recommended Audience
Project Kickoff Meeting	Large Audience
Project Status Meeting	Large Audience
Project Working Meeting	Subgroup
Project Silo Meetings	Subgroup

So, what is the difference in how a large audience meeting should be handled as opposed to a small audience meeting?

For a small audience meeting, when sending out the meeting agenda, it is okay to keep it brief, especially if the primary purpose of the meeting is to make decisions, work items out or it is a specific functional meeting.

For a large audience meeting, have as much information collected as possible **before** the meeting, and therefore, provide a more detailed agenda in the meeting update that is sent before the meeting.

Status meetings for example, should actually not be used to **collect** status but instead to report it. In other words, as the Project Manager you should have already elicited status updates from the project team members, collected all of this information and then provided it in the meeting agenda for that day.

Many times we have seen status meetings be used to collect status from individuals, and the result is a chaotic mess. No, for these meetings, have all project team members report their status the day before or day of as an absolute last resort, and then collect and present the completed information.

The status meeting, therefore, is used to **report** this status and to allow each individual team member to elaborate and add detail to what has been reported. It is then used for stakeholders to ask questions about this reported status.

If the status is not collected until this point, if the Project Manager has not had the opportunity to hear the information first, sometimes issues arise between the team member and stakeholder, and unfortunately for all involved the Project Manager is caught in the middle.

Optimize Roll Call:

For all meetings, I recommend that you implement what I refer to as the "five minute rule" which has two components.

On the front side of the meeting, plan to arrive at least five minutes early to the meeting, set up what needs to be set up and be ready for any early arrivers.

Then, start on time, at least with basic small talk. It is important to start on time to communicate to attendees that you are punctual so that hopefully they will develop habits of being on time.

So, then five minutes into the meeting, start with a summary of the agenda and then take roll call. This way, you eliminate the need for each person to identify themselves on the phone or in person.

Also, when individuals walk in to the meeting late or dial in late, try to resist the temptation to temporarily derail the meeting conversation to have them introduce themselves. This is rude to the people who arrived for the meeting on time, and should be avoided if possible.

Control The Meeting Conversations:

How many times do we schedule meetings with a clear and obvious set agenda, only to have perhaps one or two more assertive and verbose individual "hijack" a meeting and get off on to a conversational tangent?

For situations such as this it is imperative to be able to very diplomatically table these sidebar conversations and regain focus of the meeting.

Now, especially if dealing with stakeholders and management, it is important to maintain some tact when re-focusing the group. It is important to remember, the Project Manager's role is one of organization and leadership, but not dictatorship.

I worked with one Project Manager who was infamous for barking out at people for even sharing brief small talk between each other.

"No sidebar conversations!" He would bark, perhaps re-focusing the meeting, but leaving an unfavorable impression with all of those who worked on his projects.

So, what I have seen work is to politely say something to the effect of:

"Hey, for now that topic exceeds the agenda of this meeting. How about we set up a follow up meeting for us to discuss this in greater detail?"

If this polite tactic does not work, then maybe this comes down to having a smaller meeting group, which should hopefully reduce the tangents, although it is quite frankly impossible to eliminate all of them.

Meeting Minutes:

One feature that is fairly easy to overlook is the concept of Meeting Minutes. Although this seems tedious, and does temporarily make the role of Project Manager one of secretary or admin it is nonetheless very important. Over the course of the project, decisions will happen quickly, ideas will be discussed and over time the sequence of these decisions and ideas can easily be forgotten.

With well documented meeting minutes, it should be fairly easily to view these meeting minutes as a group and then identify the sequence of decisions, ideas, and action items.

For a fairly minimal effort during the meeting, we have found that this exercise can save all sorts of work and confusion later, just by having all of this documented. We should not forget how many meetings people have, and how easy it is for the topics of one to bleed over into the other and confuse our memories. A well-documented set of meeting minutes helps to alleviate this problem.

It is also classic Project Manager "CYA", so trust me on this point.

During the meeting, if it is possible, look to log key discussion points, action items and takeaways such that there is a planned next step as a result of the meeting.

As we stated earlier, a meeting should have a purpose, and with that purpose should have some kind of a result. Sometimes, the only result is the planning of more meetings, but that is still a result.

In an ideal situation, the result of a meeting would be a decision, one or more action items, and the next planned meeting.

Here is an example of a very basic Meeting Minutes document in Microsoft Word 2010

PROJECT MEETING MINUTES

PROJECT NAME:
PROJECT MANAGER:
DATE:

Attendees:

Planned Agenda Discussion Items:

_____

_____

Discussion Points/Decisions:

DISCUSSION POINTS

Now this is a super simple document that just has what is required to log what occurred in the meeting.

In this example, we have five sections; the top section serves only to introduce the basics of the project such as Project Manager, Project Name, and Meeting Date.

The additional sections are as follows:

Attendees: Now, at first glance this might appear to be superfluous. Won't people know who was/was not at the meeting? Yes, in the short term they will, but what is important here is for the long-term perspective. It might be a demonstrated pattern that a certain number of people are not making meetings yet then coming back with concerns or complaints later in the project. I have successfully defended claims from team members about not being informed by noting their absences from key meetings.

Planned Agenda Discussion Items: This would be the **planned** agenda that was sent out in the meeting announcement update mentioned in the earlier section. These planned agenda items likely deviated, but in this section mention only what was planned to be discussed.

Discussion Points/Decisions: In this section capture the key discussion points and key decisions that resulted from these discussions. Please resist the temptation to log every sidebar conversation and less relevant tangent. As a rule, the majority of these discussion points and decisions should tie back fairly obviously to one of the planned agenda discussion items.

Action Items: In our opinion, this is the most crucial element of the meeting minute document. This tells the team what is going to happen next, and the person(s) responsible for completing it. This section of the meeting minutes is invaluable for dealing with potential controversies later.

Not sure about the rest of you, but many, many times team members have denied that something was their responsibility at a later date. But when you can point to a dated email with an included meeting minutes document attached to it, that is some kind of solid evidence.

SUMMARY:

In this book, one of our core themes has been the importance of communication in project management. Meetings are nothing more than a type of communication, and therefore, should be viewed as an important component in a Project Management effort.

To optimize meetings, we recommend that they:

- Have a specific agenda
- Are targeted to the correct audience(resist temptation to invite everybody)
- Are documented with meeting minutes
- Have a clear set of Action items as a result

By following these helpful tips, meetings can be an important and productive part of the Project Management process and not just a 'necessary evil' as some people term them.

APPENDIX 2: Project Methodology Answers

In this section we will answer the questions posed earlier about which project management methodology type to use for each specific project.

Part of our main point in this book is the fact that each project needs to be evaluated on its own merits and assumptions not made too soon.

Portfolio Project 1: Server Upgrade Project --Waterfall

We recommend Waterfall here for a number of reasons. First, this is not a development project but will also involve physical servers ordered over a phased period of time. For these reasons we recommend **Waterfall**.

Now could an infrastructure project be managed in an Agile manner, yes it could. If, for example, one set of servers could be ordered, installed and configured and this is done in an iterative manner and Agile strategy could be used. Also, if the company is using virtual servers to improve capacity but are not sure how much capacity was required.

This too would be a candidate for an Agile strategy.

Portfolio Project 2: Software Patch Application --Waterfall Or Agile

This project gets the ambiguous either/or response because it will come down to how and when it needs to be completed. I would guess that most companies, however, would want to structure this very clearly in the planning phase, therefore this is likely a Waterfall project.

Portfolio Project 3: Web Page Design From Scratch --Agile

This could also be Agile PM 2020. For a from-scratch software, website etc, we recommend Agile. With very little solid requirements in place, this is a strong candidate for a full Agile or Agile PM 2020 approach.

Portfolio Project 4: Script Modifications --Waterfall

This is recommended to be Waterfall because of the relative simplicity of the project and also the individuals responsible. Since it is the offshore team doing it, go ahead and use Waterfall as the benefit of assembling an Agile team would be minimized.

Portfolio Project 5: Large Custom Software Implementation With Interfaces And Configurations --Agile Project Managment 2020

We strongly recommend Agile Project Management 2020 here as the large scope of the project will necessitate the combination of Waterfall and Agile strategies.

For the software implementation, use the Waterfall framework to cover planned activities such as vendor evaluation, etc.

For the interfaces and the configurations, assemble an Agile team and have them work completely in an Agile capacity.

Ideally, this could be done in parallel with the non-development steps to save time. As one part of the team is working on the software deployment, the Agile team can be coordinating the interfaces and the configuration requirements.

APPENDIX 3: Specific Project Types

In this appendix section, we put our philosophy to use and attempt to illustrate the specifics of various project types and then discuss how these might be managed.

Specific Project Type: Infrastructure Projects

As a rule, for all projects that follow a specified timeline, that follow a sequential order of some sort, either mandated or logical, it is best to use a Waterfall methodology for these projects. Now, please note that this is the rule but there are always exceptions to every rule, and we expect that each specific project should be evaluated as we have stressed up to this point.

For the moment, let's analyze a fairly common Infrastructure project, the need to upgrade physical hardware at a secondary location.

Other types of IT Infrastructure projects that should be approached similarly

- Set up a new physical location
- Installation of network circuits
- Data center moves
- New desktop rollouts
- Deployment of new operating systems

- Scaling servers (either physical or virtual)

This project involves, at least at the beginning, the evaluation of current infrastructure at the site and then after the evaluation of the current "as-is" infrastructure, the analysis and decision what to do next, whether to get new physical servers or go the virtual route.

After this decision has been made, the next steps are the actual ordering, installation, and configuration of the equipment.

For this project, we envision a project plan that looks something like this, and as you can likely see, it follows the Waterfall methodology.

Note our Gantt chart from Microsoft Project 2013 below (Figure 10.1)

In the preceding project plan, we have steps that follow a fairly logical sequence that do not allow for much modification along the way. In this project, it is fairly clear that the analysis needs to be done before any ordering, and it doesn't take a genius to conclude that the ordering must come before the installation, unless you are like magic or something.

Now, that is the rule, the exception might exist in cases in which the decision has been made that the hardware will be ordered en masse but then installed a few servers at a time to determine what the scaling needs are. This way, some servers could be held in reserve and scaled up later if needed. If this was the approach, then an Agile approach could be implemented, and a Scrum methodology used.

In our experience, this is highly unlikely when working with physical servers. For virtualization, which we will discuss more in detail later, this makes a great deal more sense, but not really for physical servers.

So, for a **majority** of Infrastructure projects, the AgilePM2020 recommendations are for the following:

Project Type	Infrastructure Projects
Methodology	Waterfall
Project Leads:	Project Manager and Technical Architect
Team Size:	Depends on need
Outsourcing:	Full Outsourcing is fine

Software Implementation Projects

Another very common type of project in the I.T world would be *Software Implementation Projects*.

Now, as soon as most people see the word "Software", they immediately jump to the conclusion that we should use an Agile methodology.

Not so fast.

When we mention software implementation projects, we generalize to refer to instances in which some third party software is acquired that will serve a particular business need. We are not referring to tools such as Microsoft Office, Microsoft Project or anything like that, we are referring to tools such as a vendor provided solution which could be as simple as a web-based utility, or as involved as an Enterprise ERP solution such as SAP.

Software development and software implementation are very different animals and need to be approached completely differently. Unfortunately, many times there is not a standard response as to which methodology would be the best to use in all cases. It comes down to the classic I.T idiom of:

It depends.

For the most part, software implementations should be initially managed using a Waterfall methodology, but the "depends" part of it comes down to the variable factors of how much customization will be required, and any custom coding or development that will be required to go with it. In all of my experience, I have never implemented a third party piece of software that did not at least require some configuration or interfaces or custom development of some sort.

So, even though we are Agile proponents, for projects of this type it is our recommendation that the entire project follow a Waterfall methodology. This is necessitated by the fact that all of the other steps that don't involve software development need to be coordinated and to do this and manage all of this; Waterfall is your best bet.

Again, one of the primary messages we are conveying is that each project needs to be judged on its own merit, so for an individual project with certain circumstances, Agile might work best for you.

For us, we just simply haven't seen it work well.

Here is a sample Software Implementation Project Plan Gantt Chart in Microsoft Project 2013.

		Task Mode	Task Name	Duration	Start	Finish	Predecessors
1			▲ Software Implemenation Project	126 days	Thu 11/5/15	Thu 4/28/16	
2			Phase One: Requirements	17 days	Thu 11/5/15	Fri 11/27/15	
3			Phase Two: Vendor Evaluation/RFQ	17 days	Tue 12/1/15	Wed 12/23/1	
4			Phase Three: Implementation	40 days	Mon 1/4/16	Fri 2/26/16	
5			Phase Four: Configuration	25 days	Fri 2/26/16	Thu 3/31/16	
6			Phase Five: Interfaces and Custom Development	21 days	Thu 3/31/16	Thu 4/28/16	

In our plan above, we operate from the assumption that all of the steps need to be done in a sequential order, which most logically necessitates a Waterfall approach.

Now, with the configuration, interfaces, and custom development it is quite possible that these phases can begin at least on the requirements side during the other requirements gathering phases.

It all depends on how you choose to organize your projects and how and when the resources are available to your team.

We have found it to be most efficient to gather all interface and custom development requirements identified in the early going and then ideally this should both shorten the development phase of the project, but also keep the technical team engaged early and then throughout the duration of the project.

Project Type:	Software Implementation
Methodology:	Waterfall or Agile PM 2020(Hybrid)
Project Leads:	Project Manager
Team Size:	No fixed rule
Outsourcing:	Mostly on site -Partial Outsourcing only

Software Development Projects

See if this scenario sounds familiar:

The business comes to your department with nothing but a vague idea. Maybe we can have a form that does this, or that, or whatever. For a project with such poorly-defined scope, for which the business wants a fairly quick turnaround, what should be done?

Should you attempt to follow a structured, PMI- type Waterfall approach when scope is poorly defined?

The answer is a fairly obvious "No".

Software development projects are quite obviously the most logical for an Agile approach. The dynamic nature of the requirements, the tendencies of users to not really know what they want until they see something and other factors lead us to recommend Agile and Scrum as the preferred approach for software development projects.

So, to summarize the **rule** for software development projects is AGILE. But for every rule there must be a few exceptions, right?

What then, might be some exceptions to this base rule in which a Waterfall approach might work best.

No Dedicated Team – You are probably tired of reading this, but in our estimation, there simply is no Agile without a dedicated team. An attempt can be made to do some type of pseudo-Agile, but for a truly Agile approach, the appropriate people must be both available and dedicated to the project.

Specialized Skill Sets – This is similar to the item above, a case in which the requirements involve a skill that only one or two resources in the company possess. This renders a truly Agile team useless and makes for more of a Waterfall strategy.

Strict, Mandated Timeline – If there exists a situation such that a project must be completed at a set time due to some type of external factor or timeline such as a compliance issue, then Waterfall should be considered.

We mentioned it before but it bears repeating, when some type of government or other compliance requirement is behind the project or the reason for the project, then a team might prefer the more linear structure of Waterfall than the more-dynamic Agile.

But, with these noted exceptions notwithstanding, we will present a project plan that utilizes an Agile methodology as we would advocate:

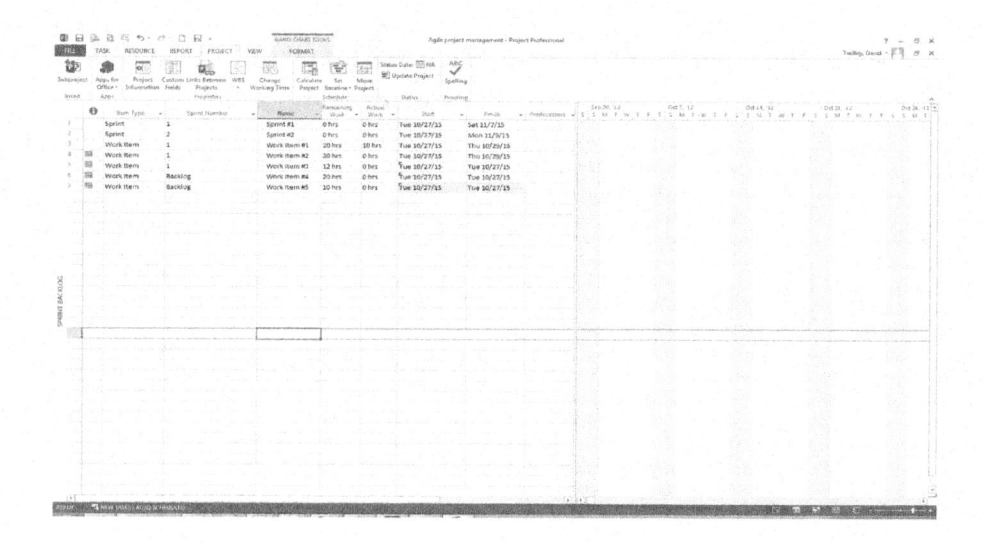

In the above example, we have set the basic sprint plan for the first two sprints, and a few additional work items.

At this point, all sprints have not yet been defined, but if there was a project with a fixed compliance and/or due date, it would be advisable to have all of those sprints planned out and the dates identified and committed.

This project plan would define each sprint based upon the Product Backlog as shown in the example below:

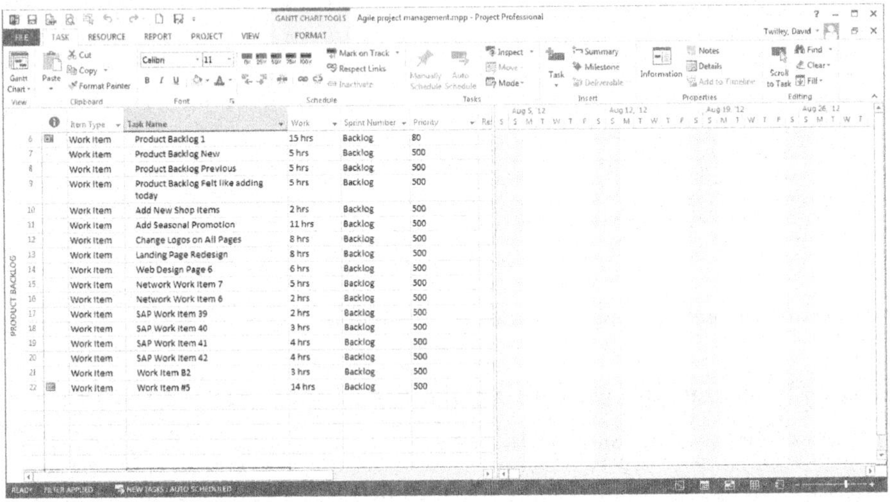
Agile project management.mpp - Project Professional
TASK RESOURCE REPORT PROJECT VIEW FORMAT
PRODUCT BACKLOG
Item Type Task Name Work Sprint Number Priority
6 Work Item Product Backlog 1 15 hrs Backlog 80
7 Work Item Product Backlog New 5 hrs Backlog 500
8 Work Item Product Backlog Previous 5 hrs Backlog 500
9 Work Item Product Backlog Felt like adding today 5 hrs Backlog 500
10 Work Item Add New Shop Items 2 hrs Backlog 500
11 Work Item Add Seasonal Promotion 11 hrs Backlog 500
12 Work Item Change Logos on All Pages 8 hrs Backlog 500
13 Work Item Landing Page Redesign 8 hrs Backlog 500
14 Work Item Web Design Page 6 6 hrs Backlog 500
15 Work Item Network Work Item 7 5 hrs Backlog 500
16 Work Item Network Work Item 6 2 hrs Backlog 500
17 Work Item SAP Work Item 39 2 hrs Backlog 500
18 Work Item SAP Work Item 40 3 hrs Backlog 500
19 Work Item SAP Work Item 41 4 hrs Backlog 500
20 Work Item SAP Work Item 42 4 hrs Backlog 500
21 Work Item Work Item 82 3 hrs Backlog 500
22 Work Item Work Item #5 14 hrs Backlog 500

This will cover the majority of project types that will be encountered in and IT environment.

If you as a reader have an unusual project type and a question as to how this project might best be managed, please don't hesitate to reach out to me at **David.Twilley@True-SpiritConsulting.com** and I may even include this case study in a future edition of this book.

APPENDIX 4: Professional Certifications

There is a wide array of professional certifications that are available to enhance your Project Management resume. For many companies, these certifications have become almost a prerequisite for many Project Management positions.

What I will do in this section is to provide the information that I have on each, and my very subjective opinion on which certification helps the most depending on where an individual is on their career path.

As noted earlier, I currently hold the PMI Project Management Professional(PMP) certification, the Scrum Alliance's Certified Scrum Master certification and a Lean Six Sigma Green Belt certification.

So, here I will discuss each of the three and one additional certification that I do not have and deliberate the advantages and disadvantages of each.

PMI Project Management Professional (PMP):

For a true project manager with several years of experience, this is the ideal certification for you. In my experience, no other certification is mandatory and required for more positions than is the PMP. I also feel that the scope of knowledge and experience required to obtain this certification makes it a more valid and useful credential for evaluating potential candidates.

Many candidates could claim to have extensive Project Management experience, but when I interview a candidate that has a PMP certification, I know that they went through a long application process and passed a very difficult examination.

The PMP certification is something which I believe all serious Project Managers should obtain, and those getting into project management should view this as being on their radar.

Pros: Industry-respected certification. Thorough examination and application process

Cons: Difficult for non-experienced Project Managers to qualify for. Does not focus on Agile concepts.

For more information on the Project Management Professional certification, please visit PMI at **www.pmi.org** to learn all about it.

The Scrum Alliance Certified Scrum Master

For all of the work that went into getting the PMP certification, the process for the CSM(Certified Scrum Master) is significantly easier.

It would be tough for me to recommend this certification for a true Project Manager, but it was worth it for me just to do the two day CSM-prep class with instructor Lee Henson. This man was able to turn a fairly dry subject into a very enjoyable two day class.

The process for getting the CSM is an open book exam at the end of the required two-day course, that is painfully easy to pass.

For this reason and the fact that I have received almost zero interest in jobs because of holding this credential leads me to not recommending it.

But, I strongly believe that a formal class is warranted and I think whether someone wanted the PMI-ACP preparation courses or Lee Henson's

Certified Scrum Master course, it is imperative to learn more about the formalities of the Scrum process.

For more information, contact the Scrum Alliance at **www.Scrumalliance.org**

Lean Six Sigma Green Belt/ Black Belt:

In preparation for the PMP exam, one of the areas that I spent the most time on was the Monitoring and Controlling section. All of the methods for control checks and validation and all of that really appealed to me.

Then in the real world, I noticed how rarely these controls and measures were ever truly implemented.

So, for that reason, the Lean Six Sigma courses had value as they focused more on things of that nature and allowed for more elaboration on those topics.

For a Project Management career, however, I have yet to truly see any significant benefit to possessing this credential. Typically, if you are seeking an Operations position or Manager of Quality Control type of position then this would help you, but not for just a Project Management job.

David B. Twilley, PMP, CSM

Top Certifications and Requirements for Each:

PMP – Project Management Professional

Fees: (As of December 2015)	For PMI Members – 405.00 USD ; For Non-Members 555.00 USD
Education & Experience Requirements:	Either **one** of the following combinations
	Four-Year Secondary Degree + 3 years of Project Management Experience
	4,500 hours directing projects
	35 Hours of Project Management education
	OR:
	High School Diploma
	5 years of Project Management experience
	7500 hours leading and directing projects
	35 hours of Project Management education

PMI-ACP

The PMI-ACP formally recognizes one's knowledge of Agile principles and one's skill with Agile technologies.

Fees: (As of December 2015)	For PMI Members – 435.00 USD ; For Non-Members 495.00 USD
Education & Experience Requirements:	2000 hours of project management experience
	1,500 hours working on Agile teams
	21 contact hours of Agile training

APPENDIX 5:   How Not To Run A Meeting:

At one of my recent projects we had a series of meetings that functioned very similar to the example that I will site below. This is a prime example on why meetings fail, and hopefully provide some motivation to correct and improve this chronic problem.

MEETING AGENDA –MONDAY -- 10AM – 1030

10:00 AM	**Kick people of conference room (politely) because their meeting ran over into your scheduled time.**
10:05	Start meeting late; finally open conference bridge phone line
10:07	Begin taking roll call; pausing several times for late arrivals, who feel the need to announce themselves even when not prompted to do so.
10:09	Politely(?) remind remote attendees to mute their phone as we don't particularly need to hear their barking dog, crying baby, or whatever TV show they are watching at the moment
10:10	Finally complete roll call

10:15	Begin meeting by summarizing the past meeting and having to repeat it for those who dial in late
10:20	Engage in new items for discussion, Ask for input from key attendees. Pause. Inform people they are on mute. Laugh awkwardly
10:30	Ignore people pressing their noses on the glass door of the conference room, waiting on you.
10:35	End meeting late, and Email content that should have been emailed prior to meeting. Schedule next meeting in series. Lather. Rinse. Repeat. Ask No Questions

APPENDIX 6: Sample Documents

PROJECT CHARTER
Project Objectives:

The AgilePM2020 website is required to enable a blog site for people and fans of the book to comment and tell us how great we are. Users should be able to post comments, articles, and order our books.

Goals

- Site must be cool looking
- Site must have a Blog
- Site must have shopping cart and download functionality

Scope

The end result of this project will be the deployment of a streamlined, functional website for AGILEPM2020. It will feature multiple pages with blog, user community, and e-commerce capabilities. Users will be able to review on-line courses, order books, and be able to discuss

David B. Twilley, PMP, CSM

Key Stakeholders

Client	[True Spirit Consulting]
Sponsor	[David B. Twilley]
Project manager	[Susan D Olson]
Project team members	[Nick Malone, Suhit Sharma, Robert Loblaw].

Project   Milestones

[Site launched with Blog functionality]

[E-Commerce Shopping Cart Added]

[Google Adwords Campaign Created and Executed]

Project   Budget

[225,000.]

**Project Methodology:

The decision was made to use AGILE for this project, as the stakeholders agree that they would prefer incremental releases

Constraints, Assumptions, Risks, and Dependencies

(Note: for now, keep on one page, as the Planning phase ends, we expect that Constraints, Assumptions, and Risks/Dependencies will have their own entire sections)

Constraints	[Need to identify the full staff of 7 members for the initial Scrum team]
Assumptions	[Key assumption is the availability of this team. If all members are not available for our time purposes, we may be forced to switch to a Waterfall methodology]

Approval   Signatures

[Name], Project Client	[Name], Project Sponsor	[Name], Project Manager

Project Scope Statement
Scope Statement

Scope Description:
The characteristics of the product, service, or result that the project is to achieve.

Success Criteria:
The business goals to be achieved by the project.

Project Deliverables:
The specific items being produced through the execution of the project.

Not In Scope:
Specifically What is NOT included in this project

Note: sometimes this section can be the most important of all. By explicitly stating any items that could be assumed, or misunderstood, a Project Manager can prevent any potential "gotchas" from coming up later in the project.

Constraints:
Limitations on the project that restrict project options (time, budget, etc.)

GLOSSARY OF TERMS

– PMI, Scrum, And Some Made Up Stuff

A

Accept -- The act of formally receiving or acknowledging something and regarding it as being true, sound, suitable, or complete.

Acceptance Criteria -- Those criteria, including performance requirements and essential conditions, which must be met before project deliverables are accepted.

Acquire Project Team -- The process of obtaining the human resources needed to complete the project.

Actual Cost (AC) -- Total costs actually incurred and recorded in accomplishing work performed during a given time period for a schedule activity or work breakdown structure component. Actual cost can sometimes be direct labor hours alone, direct costs alone, or all costs including indirect costs. Also referred to as the actual cost of work performed (ACWP). See also earned value management and earned value technique.

Actual Duration -- The time in calendar units between the actual start date of the schedule activity and either the data date of the project schedule if the schedule activity is in progress or the actual finish date if the schedule activity is complete.

Actual Finish Date (AF) -- The point in time that work actually ended on a schedule activity. (Note: In some application areas, the schedule activity is considered "finished" when work is "substantially complete.")

Actual Start Date (AS) -- The point in time that work actually started on a schedule activity.

Agile – An umbrella term for iterative, incremental software development methodologies. Agile methodologies include Scrum, Extreme Programming, Lean and Feature-Driven Development(FDD) amongst others.

Agile Project Management 2020 – Term that created by David B Twilley to refer to a hybrid Agile approach that modifies the existing Agile Scrum methods and incorporates the traditional Project Manager and includes an enhanced more technical role for the Scrum Master. Key differences between Agile Project Management 2020 and Scrum would be the pragmatic approach to project management methodologies, using both Waterfall and Agile depending on the needs of the project and depending on the availability of the right team.

Approve. The act of formally confirming, sanctioning, ratifying, or agreeing to something.

Assumptions -- Assumptions are factors that, for planning purposes, are considered to be true, real, or certain without proof or demonstration. Assumptions affect all aspects of project planning, and are part of the progressive elaboration of the project. Project teams frequently identify, document, and validate assumptions as part of their planning process. Assumptions generally involve a degree of risk.

Assumptions Analysis -- A technique that explores the accuracy of assumptions and identifies risks to the project from inaccuracy, inconsistency, or incompleteness of assumptions.

Authority -- The right to apply project resources*, expend funds, make decisions, or give approvals.

B

Backlog – A list of product requirements that are prioritized by the customer tht conveys to an Agile team the features that should be implemented first. There are two types of backlogs used with Agile projects, a Product Backlog and a Sprint Backlog. The product backlog contains the list of all of the product requirements, whereas the Sprint backlog is a sub set of the Product Backlog that only contains the list of features to be implemented for the current sprint.

Backward Pass -- The calculation of late finish dates and late start dates for the uncompleted portions of all schedule activities. Determined by working backwards through the schedule network logic from the project's end date. The end date may be calculated in a forward pass or set by the customer or sponsor. See also schedule network analysis.

Bar Chart -- A graphic display of schedule-related information. In the typical bar chart, schedule activities or work breakdown structure components are listed down the left side of the chart, dates are shown across the top, and activity durations are shown as date-placed horizontal bars.

Baseline -- The approved time phased plan (for a project, a work breakdown structure component, a work package, or a schedule activity), plus or minus approved project scope, cost, schedule, and technical changes.

Baseline Finish Date -- The finish date of a schedule activity in the approved schedule baseline. See also scheduled finish date.

Brainstorming --A general data gathering and creativity technique that can be used to identify risks, ideas, or solutions to issues by using a group of team members or subject-matter experts. Typically, a brainstorming session is structured so that each participant's ideas are recorded for later analysis.

Budget -- The approved estimate for the project or any work breakdown structure component or any schedule activity. See also estimate.

Budget at Completion (BAC) --The sum of all the budget values established for the work to be performed on a project or a work breakdown structure component or a schedule activity. The total planned value for the project.

BurnDown Chart – On this chart, units of work are tracked to determine how much work remains. It is tracked on X and Y axis, with the units of work remaining on the Y axis.

C

Chart of Accounts -- Any numbering system used to monitor project costs* by category (e.g., labor, supplies, materials, and equipment). The project chart of accounts is usually based upon the corporate chart of accounts of the primary performing organization. Contrast with code of accounts.

Close Project --The process of finalizing all activities across all of the project process groups to formally close the project or phase.

Closing Processes --Those processes performed to formally terminate all activities of a project or phase, and transfer the completed product to others or close a cancelled project.

Code of Accounts --Any numbering system used to uniquely identify each component of the work breakdown structure. Contrast with chart of accounts.

Co-location --An organizational placement strategy where the team are physically located close to one another in order to improve communication, working relationships, and productivity.

Communication --- A process through which information is exchanged among persons using a common system of symbols, signs, or behaviors.

Communication Management Plan -- The document that describes: the communications needs and expectations for the project; how and in what format information will be communicated; when and where each communication will be made; and who is responsible for providing each type of communication.

Communications Planning -- The process of determining the information and communications needs of the project stakeholders: who they are, what is their level of interest and influence on the project, who needs what information, when will they need it, and how it will be given to them.

Constraint -- The state, quality, or sense of being restricted to a given course of action or inaction. An applicable restriction or limitation, either internal or external to the project, that will affect the performance of the project or a process. For example, a schedule constraint is any limitation or restraint placed on the project schedule that affects when a schedule activity can be scheduled and is usually in the form of fixed imposed dates.

Contract -- A contract is a mutually binding agreement that obligates the seller to provide the specified product or service or result and obligates the buyer to pay for it.

Contract Administration -- The process of managing the contract and the relationship between the buyer and seller, reviewing and documenting how a seller is performing or has performed to establish required corrective actions and provide a basis for future relationships with the seller, managing contract related changes and, when appropriate, managing the contractual relationship with the outside buyer of the project.

Contract Closure -- The process of completing and settling the contract, including resolution of any open items and closing each contract.

Control -- Comparing actual performance with planned performance, analyzing variances, assessing trends to effect process improvements, evaluating possible alternatives, and recommending appropriate corrective action as needed.

Control Account (CA) -- A management control point where the integration of scope, budget, actual cost, and schedule takes place, and where the measurement of performance will occur. Control accounts are placed at selected management points (specific components at selected levels) of the work breakdown structure.

Control Chart -- A graphic display of process data over time and against established control limits, and that has a centerline that assists in detecting a trend of plotted values toward either control limit.

Control Limits -- The area composed of three standard deviations on either side of the centerline, or mean, of a normal distribution of data plotted on a control chart that reflects the expected variation in the data.

Corrective Action -- Documented direction for executing the project work to bring expected future performance of the project work in line with the project management plan.

Cost -- The monetary value or price of a project activity* or component that includes the monetary worth of the resources required to perform and complete the activity or component, or to produce the component.

Create WBS (Work Breakdown Structure) -- The process of subdividing the major project deliverables and project work into smaller, more manageable components.

Critical Activity -- Any schedule activity on a critical path in a project schedule. Most commonly determined by using the critical path method.

Although some activities are "critical," in the dictionary sense, without being on the critical path, this meaning is seldom used in the project context.

Critical Chain Method -- A schedule network analysis technique* that modifies the project schedule to account for limited resources. The critical chain method mixes deterministic and probabilistic approaches to schedule network analysis.

Critical Path -- Generally, but not always, the sequence of schedule activitiesthat determines the duration of the project. Generally, it is the longest path through the project. However, a critical path can end, as an example, on a schedule milestone that is in the middle of the project schedule and that has a finish-no-later-than imposed date schedule constraint. See also critical path method.

Critical Path Method (CPM) -- A schedule network analysis technique* used to determine the amount of scheduling flexibility (the amount of float) on various logical network paths in the project schedule network, and to determine the minimum total project duration.

Current Finish Date -- The current estimate of the point in time when a schedule activity will be completed, where the estimate reflects any reported work progress.

Current Start Date -- The current estimate of the point in time when a schedule activity will begin, where the estimate reflects any reported work progress. See also scheduled start date and baseline start date.

Customer -- The person or organization that will use the project's product or service or result.

D

Date -- A term representing the day, month, and year of a calendar, and, in some instances, the time of day.

Decision Tree Analysis -- The decision tree is a diagram that describes a decision under

Definition of Done – This is a universally-agreed upon criteria for what makes a unit of work "potentially shippable". This checklist of steps must be completed for each unit of work.

Deliverable -- Any unique and verifiable product, result, or capability to perform a service that must be produced to complete a process, phase, or project. Often used more narrowly in reference to an external deliverable, which is a deliverable that is subject to approval by the project sponsor or customer.

Develop Project Charter -- The process of developing the project charter that formally authorizes a project.

Develop Project Management Plan -- The process of documenting the actions necessary to define, prepare, integrate, and coordinate all subsidiary plans into a project management plan.

Develop Preliminary Project Scope Statement -- The process of developing the preliminary project scope statement that provides a high-level scope narrative.

Develop Project Team -- The process of improving the competencies and interaction of team members to enhance project performance.

Direct and Manage Project Execution -- The process of executing the work defined in the project management plan to achieve the project's requirements defined in the project scope statement.

E

Epic – A large user story. Epics can be decomposed into user stories as they near implementation.

Estimate -- A quantitative assessment of the most likely outcome

Execute -- Directing, managing, performing, and accomplishing the project work, providing the deliverables, and providing work performance information.

Executing Processes -- Those processes performed to complete the work defined in the project management plan to accomplish the project's objectives defined in the project scope statement.

Expected Monetary Value (EMV) Analysis -- A statistical technique that calculates the average outcome when the future includes scenarios that may or may not happen. A common use of this technique is within decision tree analysis.

F

Fast Tracking -- A specific project schedule compression technique that changes network logic to overlap phases that would normally be done in sequence, such as the design phase and construction phase, or to perform schedule activities in parallel. See schedule compression and see also crashing.

Flowcharting -- The depiction in a diagram format of the inputs, process actions, and outputs of one or more processes within a system.

Forward Pass -- The calculation of the early start and early finish dates for the uncompleted portions of all network activities. See also schedule network analysis and backward pass.

Functional Organization -- A hierarchical organization where each employee has one clear superior, staff are grouped by areas of specialization, and managed by a person with expertise in that area.

G

Gantt Chart -- similar to a Bar Chart, it is a A graphic display of schedule-related information. In the typical bar chart, schedule activities or work breakdown structure components are listed down the left side of the chart, dates are shown across the top, and activity durations are shown as date-placed horizontal bars.

Grade -- A category or rank used to distinguish items that have the same functional use (e.g., "hammer"), but do not share the same requirements for quality (e.g., different hammers may need to withstand different amounts of force).

H

Historical Information -- Documents and data on prior projects including project files, records, correspondence, closed contracts, and closed projects.

Human Resource Planning -- The process of identifying and documenting project roles, responsibilities and reporting relationships, as well as creating the staffing management plan.

I

Impediment – In Scrum and Agile Project Management 2020, an impediment is any obstacle prventing a developer or team from completing work. One of the three focusing questions each member of Scrum answers during the daily stand up meeting relates to how many impediments stand in their way. One of the key jobs of the Scrum Master is to remove impediments for the project team.

Imposed Date -- A fixed date imposed on a schedule activity or schedule milestone, usually in the form of a "start no earlier than" and "finish no later than" date.

Information Distribution -- The process of making needed information available to project stakeholders in a timely manner.

Initiating Processes -- Those processes performed to authorize and define the scope of a new phase or project or that can result in the continuation of halted project work.

Input -- Any item, whether internal or external to the project that is required by a process before that process proceeds. May be an output from a predecessor process.

Inspection -- Examining or measuring to verify whether an activity, component product, result or service conforms to specified requirements.

Integrated Change Control -- The process of reviewing all change requests, approving changes and controlling changes to deliverables and organizational process assets.

Issue -- A point or matter in question or in dispute, or a point or matter that is not settled and is under discussion or over which there are opposing views or disagreements.

Iteration – The uninterrupted period of time during which an Agile team performs work. This is most commonly two to four weeks. At the end of each iteration, the project team delivers a "potentially shippable" product as a result of this iteration. In Agile and Agile Project Management 2020, iterations typically begin with a planning meeting and end with a retrospective.

K

Knowledge -- Knowing something with the familiarity gained through experience, education, observation, or investigation, it is understanding a process, practice, or technique, or how to use a tool.

L

Lag -- A modification of a logical relationship that directs a delay in the successor activity. For example, in a finish-to-start dependency with a ten-day lag, the successor activity cannot start until ten days after the predecessor activity has finished. See also lead.

Lead -- A modification of a logical relationship that allows an acceleration of the successor activity. For example, in a finish-to-start dependency with a ten-day lead, the successor activity can start ten days before the predecessor activity has finished. See also lag. A negative lead is equivalent to a positive lag.

Lessons Learned -- The learning gained from the process of performing the project. Lessons learned may be identified at any point. Also considered a project record, to be included in the lessons learned knowledge base.

Lessons Learned Knowledge Base -- A store of historical information and lessons learned about both the outcomes of previous project selection decisions and previous project performance.

Level of Effort (LOE) -- Support-type activity (e.g., seller or customer liaison, project cost accounting, project management, etc.) that does not readily lend itself to measurement of discrete accomplishment. It is generally characterized by a uniform rate of work performance over a period of time determined by the activities supported.

M

Manage Project Team -- The process of tracking team member performance, providing feedback, resolving issues, and coordinating changes to enhance project performance.

Manage Stakeholders -- The process of managing communications to satisfy the requirements of, and resolve issues with, project stakeholders.

Master Schedule -- A summary-level project schedule that identifies the major deliverables and work breakdown structure components and key schedule milestones. See also milestone schedule.

Matrix Organization -- Any organizational structure in which the project manager shares responsibility with the functional managers for assigning priorities and for directing the work of persons assigned to the project.

Methodology -- A system of practices, techniques, procedures, and rules used by those who work in a discipline.

Milestone -- A significant point or event in the project. See also schedule milestone.

Monitor -- Collect project performance data with respect to a plan, produce performance measures, and report and disseminate performance information.

Monitor and Control Project Work -- The process of monitoring and controlling the processes required to initiate, plan, execute, and close a project to meet the performance objectives defined in the project management plan and project scope statement.

Monitoring and Controlling Processes -- Those processes performed to measure and monitor project execution* so that corrective action can be taken when necessary to control the execution of the phase or project.

Monte Carlo Analysis -- A technique that computes, or iterates, the project cost or project schedule many times using input values selected at random from probability distributions of possible costs or durations, to calculate a distribution of possible total project cost or completion dates.

N

Node -- One of the defining points of a schedule network; a junction point joined to some or all of the other dependency lines. See also arrow diagramming method and precedence diagramming method.

O

Objective -- Something toward which work is to be directed, a strategic position to be attained, or a purpose to be achieved, a result to be obtained, a product to be produced, or a service to be performed.

Operations -- An organizational function performing the ongoing execution of activities that produce the same product or provide a repetitive service. Examples are: production operations, manufacturing operations, and accounting operations.

Opportunity -- A condition or situation favorable to the project, a positive set of circumstances, a positive set of events, a risk that will have a positive impact on project objectives, or a possibility for positive changes. Contrast with threat.

Organization Chart -- A method for depicting interrelationships among a group of persons working together toward a common objective.

Output -- A product, result, or service generated by a process. May be an input to a successor process.

P

Parametric Estimating -- An estimating technique that uses a statistical relationship between historical data and other variables (e.g., square footage in construction, lines of code in software development) to calculate an estimate for activity parameters, such as scope, cost, budget, and duration.

Pareto Chart -- A histogram, ordered by frequency of occurrence, that shows how many results were generated by each identified cause.

Percent Complete (PC or PCT) -- An estimate, expressed as a percent, of the amount of work that has been completed on an activity or a work breakdown structure component.

Perform Quality Assurance (QA) -- The process of applying the planned, systematic quality activities (such as audits or peer reviews) to ensure that the project employs all processes needed to meet requirements.

Perform Quality Control (QC) -- The process of monitoring specific project results* to determine whether they comply with relevant quality standards and identifying ways to eliminate causes of unsatisfactory performance.

Performance Measurement Baseline -- An approved plan for the project work against which project execution is compared and deviations are measured for management control. The performance measurement baseline typically integrates scope, schedule, and cost parameters of a project, but may also include technical and quality parameters.

Performance Reporting -- The process of collecting and distributing performance information. This includes status reporting, progress measurement, and forecasting.

Performance Reports -- Documents and presentations that provide organized and summarized work performance information, earned value management parameters and calculations, and analyses of project work progress and status. Common formats for performance reports include bar charts, S-curves, histograms, tables, and project schedule network diagram showing current schedule status.

Plan Purchases and Acquisitions -- The process of determining what to purchase or acquire, and determining when and how to do so.

Planned Value (PV) -- The authorized budget assigned to the scheduled work to be accomplished for a schedule activity or work breakdown structure component. Also referred to as the budgeted cost of work scheduled (BCWS).

Planning Package -- A WBS component below the control account with known work content but without detailed schedule activities. See also control account.

Planning Processes -- Those processes performed to define and mature the project scope, develop the project management plan, and identify and schedule the project activities* that occur within the project.

Portfolio -- A collection of projects or programs and other work that are grouped together to facilitate effective management of that work to meet strategic business objectives. The projects or programs of the portfolio may not necessarily be interdependent or directly related.

Portfolio Management -- The centralized management of one or more portfolios, which includes identifying, prioritizing, authorizing, managing, and controlling projects, programs, and other related work, to achieve specific strategic business objectives.

Position Description -- An explanation of a project team member's roles and responsibilities.

Practice -- A specific type of professional or management activity that contributes to the execution of a process and that may employ one or more techniques and tools.

Precedence Relationship -- The term used in the precedence diagramming method for a logical relationship. In current usage, however, precedence relationship, logical relationship, and dependency are widely used interchangeably, regardless of the diagramming method used.

Predecessor Activity -- The schedule activity that determines when the logical successor activity can begin or end.

Preventive Action -- Documented direction to perform an activity that can reduce the probability of negative consequences associated with project risks*.

Probability and Impact Matrix -- A common way to determine whether a risk is considered low, moderate, or high by combining the two dimensions of a risk: its probability of occurrence, and its impact on objectives if it occurs.

Procedure -- A series of steps followed in a regular definitive order to accomplish something.

Process -- A set of interrelated actions and activities performed to achieve a specified set of products, results, or services.

Procurement Management Plan -- The document that describes how procurement processes from developing procurement documentation through contract closure will be managed.

Product -- An artifact that is produced, is quantifiable, and can be either an end item in itself or a component item. Additional words for products are materiel and goods. Contrast with result and service. See also deliverable.

Product Life Cycle -- A collection of generally sequential, non-overlapping product phases* whose name and number are determined by the manufacturing and control needs of the organization. The last product life cycle phase for a product is generally the product's product life cycles.

Product Scope -- The features and functions that characterize a product, service or result.

Program -- A group of related projects managed in a coordinated way to obtain benefits and control not available from managing them individually. Programs may include elements of related work outside of the scope of the discrete projects in the program.

Program Management -- The centralized coordinated management of a program to achieve the program's strategic objectives and benefits.

Program Management Office (PMO) -- The centralized management of a particular program or programs such that corporate benefit is realized by the sharing of resources, methodologies, tools, and techniques, and related high-level project management focus. See also project management office.

Progressive Elaboration -- Continuously improving and detailing a plan as more detailed and specific information and more accurate estimates become available as the project progresses, and thereby producing more accurate and complete plans that result from the successive iterations of the planning process.

Project -- A temporary endeavor undertaken to create a unique product, service, or result.

Project Charter -- A document issued by the project initiator or sponsor that formally authorizes the existence of a project, and provides the project manager with the authority to apply organizational resources to project activities.

Project Management (PM) -- The application of knowledge, skills, tools, and techniques to project activities* to meet the project requirements.

Project Management Body of Knowledge (PMBOK®) -- An inclusive term that describes the sum of knowledge within the profession of project management. As with other professions such as law, medicine, and accounting, the body of knowledge rests with the practitioners and academics that apply and advance it.

Project Management Plan -- A formal, approved document that defines how the projected is executed, monitored and controlled. It may be summary or detailed and may be composed of one or more subsidiary management plans and other planning documents.

Project Management Process Group -- A logical grouping of the project management processes described in the PMBOK® Guide. The project management process groups include initiating processes, planning processes, executing processes, monitoring and controlling processes, and closing processes.

Project Management Professional (PMP®) -- A person certified as a PMP® by the Project Management Institute (PMI®).

Project Management Software -- A class of computer software applications specifically designed to aid the project management team with planning, monitoring, and controlling the project, including: cost estimating, scheduling, communications, collaboration, configuration management, document control, records management, and risk analysis.

Project Management System -- The aggregation of the processes, tools, techniques, methodologies, resources, and procedures to manage a project. The system is documented in the project management plan and its content will vary depending upon the application area, organizational influence, complexity of the project, and the availability of existing systems

Project Management Team -- The members of the project team who are directly involved in project management activities. On some smaller projects, the project management team may include virtually all of the project team members.

Project Manager (PM) -- The person assigned by the performing organization to achieve the project objectives*. The Project Manager is equally important in Waterfall and Agile methodologies according to the tenets of Agile Project Management 2020.

Project Organization Chart -- A document that graphically depicts the project team members and their interrelationships for a specific project.

Project Phase -- a collection of logically related project activities*, usually culminating in the completion of a major deliverable. Project phases (also called phases) are mainly completed sequentially, but can overlap in some project situations. Phases can be subdivided into sub phases and then components; this hierarchy, if the project or portions of the project are divided into phases, is contained in the work breakdown structure.

Project Process Groups -- The five process groups required for any project that have clear dependencies and that are required to be performed in the same sequence on each project, independent of the application area or the specifics of the applied project life cycle. The process groups are initiating, planning, executing, monitoring and controlling, and closing.

Project Schedule -- The planned dates for performing schedule activities and the planned dates for meeting schedule milestones.

Project Scope Statement -- The description of the project scope, including deliverables, project objectives, project assumptions, project constraints, and a statement of work, that provides a documented basis for making future project decisions and for confirming or developing a common understanding of project scope among the stakeholders. What needs to be accomplished?

Project Team -- All the project team members, including the project management team, the project manager and, for some projects, the project sponsor.

Project Team Members -- The persons who report either directly or indirectly to the project manager, and who are responsible for performing project work as a regular part of their assigned duties.

Q

Qualitative Risk Analysis --The process of prioritizing risks for subsequent further analysis or action by assessing and combining their probability of occurrence and impact.

Quality -- The degree to which a set of inherent characteristics fulfills requirements.

Quality Management Plan -- The quality management plan describes how the project management team will implement the performing organization's quality policy.

Quality Planning -- The process of identifying which quality standards are relevant to the project and determining how to satisfy them.

Quantitative Risk Analysis -- The process of numerically analyzing the effect on overall project objectives of identified risks.

R

Reliability -- The probability of a product performing its intended function under specific conditions for a given period of time.

Requested Change -- A formally documented change request that is submitted for approval to the integrated change control process. Contrast with approved change request

Requirement -- A condition or capability that must be met or possessed by a system, product, service, result, or component to satisfy a contract, standard, specification, or other formally imposed documents. Requirements include the quantified and documented needs, wants, and expectations of the sponsor, customer, and other stakeholders.

Resource -- Skilled human resources (specific disciplines either individually or in crews or teams), equipment, services, supplies, commodities, materiel, budgets, or funds.

Resource Breakdown Structure (RBS) -- A hierarchical structure of resources by resource category and resource type used in resource leveling schedules and to develop resource limited schedules, and which may be used to identify and analyze project human resource assignments.

Result -- An output from performing project management processes and activities. Results include outcomes (e.g., integrated systems, revised process, restructured organization, tests, trained personnel, etc.) and documents (e.g., policies, plans, studies, procedures, specifications, reports, etc.). Contrast with product and service. See also deliverable.

Risk -- An uncertain event or condition that, if it occurs, has a positive or negative effect on a project's objectives. See also risk category and risk breakdown structure.

Risk Acceptance -- A risk response planning technique* that indicates that the project team has decided not to change the project management plan to deal with a risk, or is unable to identify any other suitable response strategy.

Risk Avoidance -- A risk response planning technique* for a threat that creates changes to the project management plan that are meant to either eliminate the risk or to protect the project objectives from its impact. Generally, risk avoidance involves relaxing the time, cost, scope, or quality objectives.

Risk Breakdown Structure (RBS) -- A hierarchically organized depiction of the identified project risks* arranged by risk category and subcategory that identifies the various areas and causes of potential risks. The risk breakdown structure is often tailored to specific project types.

Risk Category -- A group of potential causes of risk. Risk causes may be grouped into categories such as technical, external, organizational, environmental, or project management. A category may include subcategories such as technical maturity, weather, or aggressive estimating. See also risk breakdown structure.

Risk Identification -- The process of determining which risks might affect the project and documenting their characteristics.

Risk Monitoring and Control -- The process of tracking identified risks, monitoring residual risks, identifying new risks, executing risk response plans, and evaluating their effectiveness throughout the project life cycle.

Risk Register -- The document containing the results of the qualitative risk analysis, quantitative risk analysis, and risk response planning. The risk register details all identified risks, including description, category, cause, probability of occurring, impact(s) on objectives, proposed responses, owners, and current status. The risk register is a component of the project management plan.

Risk Response Planning -- The process of developing options and actions to enhance opportunities and to reduce threats to project objectives.

Root Cause Analysis -- An analytical technique used to determine the basic underlying reason that causes a variance or a defect or a risk. A root cause may underlie more than one variance or defect or risk.

S

Schedule Activity -- A discrete scheduled component of work performed during the course of a project. A schedule activity normally has an estimated duration, an estimated cost, and estimated resource requirements. Schedule activities are connected to other schedule activities or schedule milestones with logical relationships, and are decomposed from work packages.

Schedule Control -- The process of controlling changes to the project schedule.

Schedule Development -- The process of analyzing schedule activity sequences, schedule activity durations, resource requirements, and schedule constraints to create the project schedule.

Schedule Management Plan -- The document that establishes criteria and the activities for developing and controlling the project schedule. It is contained in, or is a subsidiary plan of, the project management plan. The schedule management plan may be formal or informal, highly detailed or broadly framed, based on the needs of the project.

Scope -- The sum of the products, services, and results to be provided as a project. See also project scope and product scope.

Scope Change -- Any change to the project scope. A scope change almost always requires anadjustment to the project cost or schedule.

Scope Control -- The process of controlling changes to the project scope.

Scope Creep -- Adding features and functionality (project scope) without addressing the effects on time, costs, and resources, or without customer approval.

Scope Definition -- The process of developing a detailed project scope statement as the basis for future project decisions.

Scope Planning -- The process of creating a project scope management plan.

Scope Verification -- The process of formalizing acceptance of the completed project deliverables.

Select Sellers -- The process of reviewing offers, choosing from among potential sellers, and negotiating a written contract with a seller.

Seller -- A provider or supplier of products, services, or results to an organization.

Sensitivity Analysis -- A quantitative risk analysis and modeling technique used to help determine which risks have the most potential impact on the project. It examines the extent to which the uncertainty of each project element affects the objective being examined when all other uncertain elements are held at their baseline values. The typical display of results is in the form of a tornado diagram.

Service -- Useful work performed that does not produce a tangible product or result, such as performing any of the business functions supporting production or distribution. Contrast with product and result. See also deliverable.

Skill -- Ability to use knowledge, a developed aptitude, and/or a capability to effectively and readily execute or perform an activity.

Specification Limits -- The area, on either side of the centerline, or mean, of data plotted on a control chart that meets the customer's requirements for a product or service. This area may be greater than or less than the area defined by the control limits.

Spike – A task aimed at gathering information rather than at producing shippable product. A spike is a story whose purpose is to provide an answer or a solution. Like any other story or task, the spike is then given an estimate and included in the product backlog.

Sponsor -- The person or group that provides the financial resources, in cash or in kind, for the project.

Stakeholder -- Persons and organizations such as customers, sponsors, performing organization and the public, that are actively involved in the project, or whose interests may be positively or negatively affected by execution or completion of the project. They may also exert influence over the project and its deliverables.

Standard -- A document established by consensus and approved by a recognized body that provides, for common and repeated use, rules, guidelines or characteristics for activities or their results, aimed at the achievement of the optimum degree of order in a given context.

Stand-Up Meeting – This a short daily, all-hands meeting in which members of an Agile team address three key questions and then move on with their day:

--What did you get done since the last stand up?

--What will you do before the next stand up?

--What impediments stand in your way?

David B. Twilley, PMP, CSM

This meeting is held at the same time and the same place every day, with members either in a small circle or sitting at their desks.

Start Date -- A point in time associated with a schedule activity's start, usually qualified by one of the following: actual, planned, estimated, scheduled, early, late, target, baseline, or current.

Statement of Work (SOW) -- A narrative description of products, services, or results to be supplied.

System -- An integrated set of regularly interacting or interdependent components created to accomplish a defined objective, with defined and maintained relationships among its components, and the whole producing or operating better than the simple sum of its components.

T

Target Completion Date (TC). An imposed date that constrains or otherwise modifies the schedule network analysis.

Target Finish Date (TF). -- The date that work is planned (targeted) to finish on a schedule activity.

Target Schedule -- A schedule adopted for comparison purposes during schedule network analysis, which can be different from the baseline schedule. See also baseline.

Target Start Date (TS) -- The date that work is planned (targeted) to start on a schedule activity.

Task -- A term for work whose meaning and placement within a structured plan for project work varies by the application area, industry, and brand of project management software.

Three-Point Estimate -- An analytical technique that uses three cost or duration estimates to represent the optimistic, most likely, and pessimistic scenarios. This technique is applied to improve the accuracy of the estimates of cost or duration when the underlying activity or cost component is uncertain.

Threshold -- A cost, time, quality, technical, or resource value used as a parameter, and which may be included in product specifications. Crossing the threshold should trigger some action, such as generating an exception report.

Tool -- Something tangible, such as a template or software program, used in performing an activity to produce a product or result.

Total Quality Management (TQM) -- A common approach to implementing a quality improvement program within an organization.

Trend Analysis -- An analytical technique that uses mathematical models to forecast future outcomes based on historical results. It is a method of determining the variance from a baseline of a budget, cost, schedule, or scope parameter by using prior progress reporting periods' data and projecting how much that parameter's variance from baseline might be at some future point in the project if no changes are made in executing the project.

Triggers -- Indications that a risk has occurred or is about to occur. Triggers may be discovered in the risk identification process and watched in the risk monitoring and control process. Triggers are sometimes called risk symptoms or warning signs.

Triple Constraint -- A framework for evaluating competing demands. The triple constraint is often depicted as a triangle where one of the sides or one of the corners represent one of the parameters being managed by the project team.

U

User -- The person or organization that will use the project's product or service. See also customer.

User Story – An Agile requirement broken down to a simple sentence or two. This is ideally expressed from the user's point of view, and describes a unit of functionality. A user story should fit on a note card and be very brief. The product backlog is comprised of a list of user stories.

V

Validation -- The technique of evaluating a component or product during or at the end of a phase or project to ensure it complies with the specified requirements. Contrast with verification.

Variance -- A quantifiable deviation, departure, or divergence away from a known baseline or expected value.

Variance Analysis -- A method for resolving the total variance in the set of scope, cost, and schedule variables into specific component variances that are associated with defined factors affecting the scope, cost, and schedule variables.

Verification -- The technique of evaluating a component or product at the end of a phase or project to assure or confirm it satisfies the conditions imposed. Contrast with validation.

W

Waterfall – The traditional method for developing and delivering software. The waterfall method breaks a project down into discrete stages:

Work -- Sustained physical or mental effort, exertion, or exercise of skill to overcome obstacles and achieve an objective.

Work Breakdown Structure (WBS) -- A deliverable-oriented hierarchical decomposition of the work to be executed by the project team to accomplish the project objectives and create the required deliverables. It organizes and defines the total scope of the project. Each descending level represents an increasingly detailed definition of the project work. The WBS is decomposed into work packages.

Work Breakdown Structure Component -- An entry in the work breakdown structure that can be at any level.

Index

A

Actual Costs, 56, 58
agile manifesto, 70
Agile Project Management 2020, 157
Appreciate, 23

B

Burndown Chart, 86

C

Cause and Effect Diagram, 59, 60
CLOSING, 31, 63
Communicate, 21
COMMUNICATION, 126
Communication Management, 35
Control Chart, 59, 60
CONTROLLING/MONITORING, 31

D

Delegate, 22

E

Earned Value, 56, 58
EXECUTING, 31

F

Flow Chart, 59

H

Human Resource Management, 33

I

INITITATING, 31

M

Motivate, 22

O

Outsourcing, 110, 111, 115, 217, 219

P

Planned Value, 56, 57, 58
PLANNING, 31
Planning Poker, 82, 84
Portfolio/PMO Manager, 162
Product Backlog, 74, 79, 80, 222
Product Owner, 9, 74, 75, 76, 78, 79, 80, 81, 88, 141
Project Manager, 20
Project Managers, 7, 8, 9, 11, 19, 20, 21, 22, 23, 24, 34, 35, 56, 71, 78, 83, 90, 126, 127, 132, 142, 145, 197, 198

Q

Quality Management, 36

R

Risk Management, 36
Run Chart, 59

S

Scatter Diagrams, 59
Scrum, 9, 10, 11, 25, 53, 71, 73, 74, 75, 76, 77, 78, 79, 80, 81, 82, 84, 87, 88, 89, 92, 101, 141, 142, 157, 158, 198, 216, 220, 232
Scrum Master, 9, 10, 75, 76, 78, 79, 80, 81, 88, 89, 92, 141, 142, 158, 198
Sprint Planning Meeting, 74
Sprint Review Meeting, 75

T

The 8 Wastes, 90
The 80/20 Rule, 102
The Sprint Backlog, 74, 80
The Team, 77
THE WATERFALL MODEL, 30

V

Velocity, 85

BOOK REVIEW REQUEST:

If you enjoyed this book and found it useful, which hopefully you did, please spread the word and let everyone know how much you enjoyed it.

If you post a (mostly) positive review on Amazon, Goodreads, or other reputable location, please email us the following information and we will provide you a set of **100 PMP Exam sample questions** for free, plus our sincere appreciation.

Thank you all in advance.

Email the following details to
BookReviews@True-SpiritConsulting.com

Review Location:
Review Text:
Name:
E-Mail Address:

Thanks yet again.

David B. Twilley

About The Author:

David B. Twilley, PMP, CSM, Six Sigma Green Belt

David is both a traditional and agile project manager with an extensive background in Information Technology. His background includes development work, coding, DBA work, web design and other areas.

His experience with multiple industries and types of organizations has provided him with great insights as to the realistic approach for project management. It is through this extensive experience that the Agile Project Management 2020 idea was formed.

David earned his Bachelor of Science from the University of Houston, and went on to a career as a developer using such tools as Java, Visual Basic and .NET. Breaking into Project Management, he quickly saw areas that could be improved with the status quo and aimed to write about it.

As a Project Manager, he has worked extensively with both Waterfall and Agile methodologies, and is equally comfortable with both. He has seen many companies implement one methodology over the other for no apparent reason.

The Agile Project Manager 2020

Forming True Spirit Consulting, Inc a company with the vision of managing projects the way that the customer needs them to be run, rather than some bias towards a specific methodology just because that's the way it's supposed to be done.

As a writer, David has written several fictional works, including a recently published novel, *Let Vengeance Be Mine,* along with several works for both the large and the small screen.

When not writing or working on Project Management, David coaches youth baseball, develops web sites, and plays tennis and golf (poorly).

You can learn more about David at his website

http://www.davidbtwilley.com/ or at his corporate site of www.true-spiritconsulting.com